## INTROD

Have you ever danced with the devil and parachuted in the moonlight? Juggled work with play? Tried to keep a romance alive whilst working as a swordsman on a Hollywood set? In 1995, Steve was trying to figure out how to take a degree in London, keep up with his military training, and learn to sail.

A trip across the Atlantic to the Caribbean at the end of the year was an opportunity that he couldn't pass up. He had little ability on the water despite once infiltrating an English seaside village at night wearing a drysuit. Will he pass his exam, keep his girlfriend happy, get to the tropics and find a job, or will he end up in the doldrums?

A timeless coming of age story.

# FOREWORD

The events in this book are all true, they actually happened. Many characters are composites, and names have been changed. There is a glossary of sailing terms at the back, which the reader might want to consult if they find a sailing or military term they are not familiar with. The intricacies of sailing are not to all tastes. I hope I have got around that.

# 1 SCOTLAND IS THE ANSWER

As the 9.10 am Intercity 225 from Euston pulls into Glasgow's Queen Street, I stand up and stretch for my Lowe Alpine backpack, and walk slowly down the aisle, careful not to bump anyone's heads. Alighting into a Glasgow afternoon, I head through the ticket barrier to the concourse and look for my meet and greet. I spy a woman looking expectantly for northbound travellers from England, and our eyes meet.

"Hello, Steve. I'm Jane. Clyde Sailing. How was your journey?" she says, holding out her hand.

We shake hands, and she leads me to a Ford Mondeo station wagon, which she has left in a loading zone, hazards on, and we get in before the parking inspector can write us up a ticket. Jane clunks the car into "Drive" and pulls away.

"Let's hope the traffic is OK," she says breezily.

"Can't be any worse than the M25," I reply.

She smiles.

How much do I know about Scotland?

"It's the answer to everyone's holiday problems, if you overlook the weather and the midges," I had read in a magazine article. It's not warm enough now for the infamous midges, but the rain appears to be holding off. Apart from that, if I leave aside for now the Loch Ness Monster, single malt whisky, Hadrian's Wall (in England, I recall), and the screening of *Monarch of the Glen* on TV, then I soon run out of things to count.

We coast to a set of lights. Jane studies the traffic at the red-light through a set of bifocals which have a beaded metal strap that go around her neck. She takes a new underhand grip on the wheel and waits to turn right. When the light changes, we head out of the city centre. She navigates the main road, taking care to stick to the posted speed limit.

If you study a map of Glasgow on the west side of Scotland, left as you look it, you will find the River Clyde. Our route takes us along the Firth of Clyde—the mouth of the river—which opens out to an island archipelago. The well-known island of Arran sits in these waters, and the drooping Mull of Kintyre peninsula is further to the west, fronting up to the North Sea and Ireland. We approach Helensburgh, which is at an inlet on the northern bank of Garelochhead, home to the Royal Navy's submarine base— and pull up at Rhu yacht marina on the town's foreshore.

Jane enters the marina and with a creak from the suspension, parks up nose facing out to the water.

"Here we are," she says.

I can see across to the far shore without getting out of the car. Deep forests climb towards hillsides, it's a touch reminiscent of the photos I have seen of Sweden. It's cool, and a breeze ripples the water. I remember the warmer waters of the Gulf Stream flow from the Gulf of Mexico all the way up here, so palm trees grow out in the western isles.

Jane leads the way down the jetty between small fishing skiffs, and then towards yachts moored alongside. Yacht *Heavenly* is at a mooring on the far side, climbing the rising tide.

I look at her. She is 37 feet in length, Jane says, and can sleep eight comfortably.

A single mast rises several metres up into the sky. There's no sign of any sail or canvas, as they must be stowed—she might as well be naked. She has a white fiberglass hull with a smart teak trim all around the cabin. I notice a gleaming alloy wheel at the back for steering—a smaller boat might incorporate a tiller —and a domed, perspex housing with a compass. Two shiny winches either side of the cockpit hint at serious business to come.

I spot a man bent over a compartment under one seat. He hears us coming and stands up, holding out his hand.

"James Caddington."

We exchange pleasantries. I know from reading the course brochure that he is a retired lieutenant commander. He's about six feet, manages a slight stoop, and has a classic TV "Captain

Birdseye" beard. Overall, he pulls off a less athletic Sean Connery. He comes across as an agreeable gent and nods kindly and sagely.

"Steve. Good to see you. You're the first to arrive. We've just got back from the Med. Come on board and stow your gear away."

"You're for'ard Steve," he adds.

I know this means the bow, up front. He ducks inside the cabin and gestures to the berth I will use throughout my time onboard. I drop my pack onto the clean fitted sheet. Light filters through rectangular windows towards the rear, and smaller, round ones forward. Portholes? Looking around, I spot a small cooktop in the galley and a door to what must be the bathroom. There's a tiny desk with a chart of the Clyde, our playground for the coming days, and a photo of James's children in a corner nook.

Back on deck, my One2One mobile phone rings. It's from Rachael, but I can't hear what she says.

"I'm on the boat. Can't hear you," I say, shifting to a better place for reception.

"Still can't hear *you*. Call you later, Steve," she replies.

"OK."

She hangs up.

*I can't see us getting better reception out here.* But I'll give it a shot at getting in contact.

RHU MARINA

## 2 GROWING UP

I can't say I have ever distinguished myself on the water apart from managing to swim 200 metres without stopping at the local baths in London, aged ten, and even then, I built up to it over the summer holidays.

"Eight laps of the pool—don't get wet!" my father crowed.

In all fairness, you did get a badge to sew on to your swimming shorts every 50 metres, so it wasn't worth doing all in one go in any case. Mum sewed the badge on with a fine needle and a thimble over her index finger. From then onwards, my water skills were in decline. Maybe it was the fat verruca my classmates got which was off-putting, seeing boys being carried on lifeguards' shoulders back to the changing rooms. The pool was called, illustriously, "Teddington Poo"—the "l" had long gone. It might have dropped off or been stolen, but nobody bothered to replace it until I reached adolescence.

One summer, I got kicked out of the pool for what I thought was boyish horseplay. The head lifeguard didn't see it that way, and dragged me from the changing rooms, past reception and left me dripping in the street with my towel and bag thrown after me. Despite me kicking and pushing my tormenter, man overpowered boy. He wouldn't get away with that behaviour today.

I had an unremarkable childhood, not one which readily reached out to the water, or the land, or air, for that matter. My grandfather was a Canon of Christchurch in the Oxford Diocese of the Church of England, "the wooden spoon for not being made a Bishop" he joked—so early memories was mass in various places in the Home Counties, including at a convent we visited a fair bit. The nuns and the mother superior sat around talking to my mother and granny about all sorts of things—for all I knew, the comings and goings, and proclivities, of clerics and parishioners. At the dining table, I was privy to adult conversations about ecumenical matters which went over my head, but also to what was hot on the parish council.

I shared the role of head chorister with my twin brother until aged 13, when during a Saturday wedding in June my voice cracked and gave out. The poor bride looked around to see me falter, and I never went back. My treble voice was gone for good. My parents separated, and my mother's new partner was also a cleric and a product of Oxford. His booming bass-baritone voice turned heads in the local shops when he came to visit and impressed me no end.

We were living in Teddington, in south-west London. School was four miles down the road in Sunbury, and my brother and I got the train come rain or shine. One winter's day, snow fell heavily, public transport was cancelled, and we walked home in our blazers through melting snowdrifts. The school had a handful of rugby pitches, but also a pool where we could swim lengths. If I had been chucked out of the pool at the public baths, here was the opportunity to be chucked in by the masters fully clothed, if we had forgotten our bathers. I had to sit in sodden trousers in lessons a few times until I had learnt my lesson.

My mother encouraged my brother and I to read the *Swallows and Amazons* books by Arthur Ransome. These were as life-affirming to me as *The Famous Five* books had been in primary. They were set in the Lake District, or on the Norfolk Broads, and I marvelled at the way the young, confident kids learnt to sail dinghies and had lots of adventures. They spent all their time unchaperoned by helicopter parents, the world their oyster. It seemed remarkable to a ten-year-old living on the outskirts of London in the early 1980s.

Sailing wasn't a sport my parents were familiar with, though, so when my brother asked whether he could sign up to sail with school one summer, my parents went all in and funded it. He came back from a week having sailed Lasers and Mirrors, talking about points of sail, tacking, a curious practice called "gybing" and was now an authority on the use of centreboards. I was impressed, and regretted the "highbrow" journalism course I had taken, which saw me waste a week scurrying around local businesses looking for a scoop.

I was a good athlete. I could run the middle distances the boys in my house couldn't be bothered to run (more fool me) so was picked for the house events and District. Flying around the track before school, my timekeeper schoolmate timed me close to the school record.

By age 14, I was up at 5:30am and running around the neighbourhood delivering newspapers. In winter, the bitter air froze my fingers rigid, and the pain of a letterbox slamming shut on them was something else. My round took me to the grand houses which subscribed to the large broadsheets. My paper bag was stuffed with *The Daily Telegraph* and *The Times*, yet I managed the weight. Often, the papers sprawled across the street, and I had to scurry around to pick them all up, the clock ticking away eating into the time I had to get to school.

A year later, by 15, I was as fit as a butcher's dog and enjoying the physical side of life. My interest in my GCSEs was flagging, but I got enough passes "C" and above to progress to three GCE Advanced levels at the local college a bus-ride away. I had winged my exams that summer, much to the amazement of my teachers.

"You must be a genius," my form-tutor exclaimed, looking at me with disbelief and resentment.

I could only shrug. A levels were an opportunity to work out what I might be good at—English and History seemed a start.

What to do, to keep occupied in the meantime over those further years of education? I saw an advert in *Combat & Survival* magazine for paratroopers in the Army Reserve based not far from Sloane Square. With a friend of mine from down the road, I joined up at 17, the youngest they would take us—it might have been that when we had passed training, we would have been adult soldiers of 17 and a half.

It was no secret paras were elite soldiers, the cream of the infantry. I was still callow, barely 60 kilogrammes of lean muscle, but could run three miles in about 19 minutes, which I thought was a fair lick. We had to show athleticism in the entrance test, a run along a boxed course on both sides of the River Thames. The route took us past Chelsea Barracks and the Queen's Guards, and over Chelsea and Battersea bridges. One bloke ran it in a smidge under 18 minutes flat and we named him "Billy Whizz".

Parachute Regiment soldiers, like Royal Marines, are fiercely proud of their cap badge and maroon beret. The beret colour was chosen by none other than the wife of General Browning in the Second World War—novelist Daphne du Maurier. Unlike other infantry regiments, paras are required to pass a special, demanding course of speed marching, assault courses, boxing matches, and racing in teams with logs and 100 kilogramme weights over distances. This tests stamina, endurance, aggression—and courage, too. Physical ability itself was not enough.

Before my 17th year was out, still legally a minor, not even able to vote, I had qualified as an elite soldier (reservist). I had appeared in two TV documentaries, ITV's *The World In Action*, when the battalion parachuted onto Salisbury Plain, and another showcasing our training. I had stood on parade to mark the 50th anniversary of Airborne forces and had waited for the Prince of Wales (now King) our Commander-in-Chief, to inspect us. He had a broken, but mending, arm in a sling, but no one he stopped at mentioned it, nor did he say a word about my ragged parachutist's smock I had ripped on the assault course that morning. The newspapers reported he had broken the arm in a polo accident weeks before.

In 1991, a UK armoured division was sent to the Gulf and our parachuting was suspended, which delayed training—it was frustrating—and a fire broke out at the parachute factory. I bit my tongue, and we found other things to do.

We travelled to Holland to do the famous *Vierdaagse* "Four Days" march, held annually for civilians and soldiers. We had to cover

25 miles a day, 100 miles in total, through the pristine, but flat Dutch countryside. Two of us met a pair of Dutch girls with their sisters out in town one night, and the older girls agreed to a Friday night date. The next day, we marched into camp, and they were waiting near the gates, so we doubled back later in our uniforms and chatted. On the night, my date presented me with a flower and kissed me twice on both cheeks. The evening went well. We laughed on the rides of the fun fair and she inched closer. Later, in a park, I stole a kiss with my Dutch beauty.

We drove back to the channel ports the next day, me dozing and clutching my flower, properly loved up. Feeling amorous, I returned to stay with her and her family a month later. We enjoyed our time—we rode along the bicycle tracks and swam in a nearby lake and cuddled on the banks. We took the train up to Amsterdam and walked the streets, and got off the train at Arnhem on the way back, asking directions to the bridge that I had seen in the 1970s movie *A Bridge Too Far*. She sprawled on the grass embankment resting, and I took a photograph of the remembrance plaque at the entry.

It wasn't long before parachuting was reinstated. After completing seven jumps, several with equipment—we carried jerry cans weighed down with gravel—I qualified as a military parachutist, and I was proud to be awarded parachute wings. In truth, I was terrified, but it was all about containing that fear, and putting the training to practice. Nonetheless, I asserted I would parachute into Holland, as per the training schedule, with a box of chocolates in the autumn to land at my girlfriend's feet. My stepfather thought this idea was impressive and guffawed from his chair before going back to *The Times*.

# 3 HIGHER CALLINGS

By the time I got to university, an ex-polytechnic slam-bang in the middle of London, I was a self-confident young man, perhaps brash at times. I'd enrolled on a Law and International Relations degree and figured the study would help me keep my options open, as it combined the rigour and letter of the law with the softer side of the humanities. In the mix, a semester of Economics—but also Psychology, to ring the changes. An administrative officer in my regiment who processed our paperwork said that if the military category "FE" stood for further education and "HE" for higher education, then "FA" was reserved for the people who had done neither.

The first weeks at university went by in a flash. I signed up with the Equestrian club and rode during the week and kept up Army reserve training at the weekends out in Wales, Norfolk, or even Kent closer to home, one full-on weekend a month, maybe two. We enjoyed drinks down the King's Road in Chelsea, and watched the "Sloane Rangers" waltz past the clothing stores and boutiques checking their reflections in the windows.

There was talk of a trip to Kenya, and other exciting things beckoned on the programme. We spent time in southern Germany, near Hammelberg, Frankfurt—laden with packs we patrolled the dense forests—the only way to cool down was to collect water from a river with a helmet and pour it over our heads.

In my last year at university, I was in my 21$^{st}$ year. I was coxing the girl's rowing team, although again, I didn't distinguish myself (there's a pattern here). We had a training camp in Switzerland out on the SarnerSee near Lucerne, tried skiing at the local resort, and got burnt to a crisp. I didn't get wet at all, even when we rowed on the river Thames tideway between Putney and Wandsworth in London.

Over a drink in the club bar, one autumn evening, one rower, also a keen yachtsman, talked about crewing, which sounded like fun. He had shifted boats to and from the Mediterranean for clients. No money changed hands, there was no cost to the crew other than travel fees, and food. In fact, it was possible to crew your way around the world, taking advantage of the seasons and prevailing winds. I thought it sounded great, but I thought no more of it.

Not long after, I was studying for a Law exam—Employment law, more's the pity, in the Richmond public library, and took a break from the monotony of case law and precedent.

Someone had left out the seminal book *Working your way around the World* in the cubicle next to me, and when I reached for it, it fell open at a page containing a blazing photo of a yacht at sea, an island in the background. A closer look at the accompanying caption showed this was the Caribbean Sea, and that there were opportunities for crewing across the Atlantic from Africa. It sounded intriguing and matched the illustrious deeds my friend had talked about. I mailed a postcard to an address to register interest to see what would happen.

A light bulb flickered on in my head, and I decided there and then I needed to learn to sail. A little investigation on the internet shed light on a place up in Scotland that would certify me over a week living onboard in the spring.

*\*\*\**

So, my goal was to complete a Competent Crew course and, at the end of my final year, pick up a boat cruising from the Canary Islands off the coast of Morocco to Saint Lucia, an island in the Windward chain.

The yachting fraternity decides where they will cruise depending on climate—warm preferably, and the weather, preferably not blowing off the tops of the trees. There are hurricanes in the tropics from May to October, so the community decamps from the Mediterranean as stable winter sets in the Caribbean before Christmas. They'll winter out there in these latitudes before the return of the storms, leaving to return for the northern summer. To get across the Atlantic Ocean, they take advantage of the trade winds, breezes blowing from Africa, west to the Caribbean. It doesn't take a genius to work out these winds are named after the same that took old ships across in the "Age of Sail".

Later, more yachts made the crossing together—there was safety in numbers when you may only be a radio call away from help. It became an event. By the coming 1995 event, the Atlantic Rally for Cruisers would have reached their 10th anniversary.

The distance is 2,700 nautical miles (3,000 miles give or take) and boats in the flotilla manage it in as little as three weeks or take their time and do it in six—the largest 'Maxi' yachts race across inside two. The tiniest boats make the attempt. In the mix; parents with children, retirees, many for the umpteenth time, but also adventurers and opportunists like me. I'm sure I've read somewhere babies have been born mid-Atlantic.

And, I could hear the Caribbean call my name. There used to be an advert for Bacardi rum showing in the cinemas. It portrayed summer nights from a beach, with revellers partying and schmoozing, and even a colourful parrot. For many of us Brits, warm weather was a break from the ravages of winter, and we scanned travel agent's windows for cheap flights and packages in the Mediterranean to escape the overcast sky and drizzle. Never mind that the Isles of Scilly were sunny, and TV showed us Florida, and *Miami Vice,* and luxurious destinations like the Maldives. The Caribbean was something else. I *had* to go.

# 4 FORMING UP

**B**ut the Firth of Clyde is a long way north of the Caribbean, and if I was ever going to get there at the end of the year, I had to be sure to impress the Commander. It's not only me as cabin boy on *Heavenly*—I'm at the bottom of the pecking order of a group, experience wise.

James suggests we wait for the others at the pub overlooking the marina.

A small group form up, drink in hand. James sips from a pint of stout and briefs us. It's a chance to face questions directed at him, which he answers unfazed. He wears an old blue jumper with shoulder patches and a cravat, and clutches a dog-eared Filofax and sits with his back to the door. He greets regulars as they arrive and nods at them as they leave.

Eric and Mark turn up and introduce themselves. They are from the North of England, both dressed in matching sailing chic—Musto windbreakers, stone-washed jeans and brown deck shoes. It looks like Mark's are recently bought, not quite having the patina that Eric's have acquired. Eric says he is an accountant, and Mark is at Durham University. They arrived in a Series Two Land Rover, also with a natural patina of crumpled panels and a spot of rust around the door sills.

Garry is from Weybridge, Surrey, he tells us. He keeps his arms folded across his chest and leans forward enthusiastically all the time. He has a boat at Southampton on the south coast and gets out on the Solent whenever he can with his wife.

We've signed up for the "Competent Crew" course which means that by the end we can be of use to a skipper. Hauling ropes, adjusting sheets and taking turns at the wheel steering a compass bearing, that sort of thing. It doesn't make us experts, just useful members under supervision, as James takes pains to explain.

Eric, who is rather more ambitious, aims to complete the

supervisory hours he needs to be a "Day Skipper", so that he can take his own boat out on the waterways by himself.

And there's me: from south-west London, wearing a t-shirt, North Face red fleece and trainers—the odd one out there—with an ambitious plan, and resolve.

James tells us about his service in the Navy as a young officer of the watch on a destroyer and later, captain of a small minesweeper. He retired after the Falklands war, but didn't get down south to the frigid Atlantic, being elsewhere in the Mediterranean at the time (which he appears to rue as a lost opportunity). Perhaps he didn't enjoy the same meteoric rise that other Falklands veterans did, but he looks like he has many more miles in him yet.

"So, the Clyde," he calls out. "Who's been here before?"

He looks around. It's only Garry who has been up, so I figure he's our old sweat for the trip. For the rest of us, it's the first time in these waters. James says that, in his opinion, we are in one of the best places to sail, least of all learn.

"I have sailed throughout the Clyde, the Med, the North Sea and Channel. She has served me well."

He pauses. "We are a teaching boat and wherever you are at, I promise you will all progress in some way with me this week."

The last to arrive is Claire, who I can't help but notice, as she's about my age and pretty. She takes the vacant seat next to me, hooking her brunette hair behind her ear. She's also shod in a natty pair of blue deck shoes.

"Sorry I'm late," she announces. "Got out of Luton late, I'm afraid, and got stuck in Birmingham rush hour—then my car overheated."

James smiles at her.

"Ah—you must be our medical student, Claire—take a seat with the crew."

He carries on, not minding the interruption.

"Get yourself a drink. You haven't missed much," he adds.

She walks over to the bar self-consciously, orders a half pint of bitter and brings it back, depositing the glass and her car keys with a jangle on the table.

James continues,

"So, we will embark from Rhu tomorrow morning at 8am on the high tide and head towards Rothesay. My plan is open. Destinations will largely depend on prevailing winds and I'm open to suggestions."

Garry nods appreciatively.

James tells Claire her berth is the vacant slot at the bow of the boat next to mine, and we push our chairs back. I grab her bag and sling it over my shoulder. The evening is cooling. It's pitch black outside, and we see low-lying cloud over the marina, and a quickening wind—an "onshore" breeze. I shiver briefly, and tug on the zip of my fleece.

After fussing with sleeping bags, and checking the fit of our sheets, we retire to bed early, so we can be refreshed and ready for the morning.

Lying in the bow, I placed my clasped hands under my neck, elbows locked out. James sits at the table and confers with Eric and Garry, whispering, before getting up quietly.

I can't sleep, and ruminate about the week to come, listening to the night noises in the marina carrying across the water. A rowing dinghy goes past, carrying a returning couple back from the pub, and I can hear the dunk as well-managed oars make impact. Clunks sound from a nearby boat, and a light turns on and off. The smell of the sea and the shore, and a mustiness pervades the bow.

*How will I go. Will I pick up the skills? No doubt.* But the main reason I can't sleep is because of Rachael. I can't stop thinking about her.

# 5 RACHAEL

*R*achael. Last time I saw her, she had been dressed in black; a sweatshirt, denims, and ankle boots. A vivacious bubbly brunette with bouncy hair, porcelain cheeks and stunning blue eyes, she's returned home after years in Bermuda to live in Gloucestershire. All I know is that she's back out West, helping out with the family marketing business and the farm while I'm up here on a boat with a bunch of strangers.

I met her in Madrid a couple of years back when a school friend and I took an Interrail train trip around Western Europe, when Eastern Europe was still exotic. 175 pounds covered the lot, including the countries of the Eastern bloc that were just opening up. We had headed to Spain first, and felt we were being boiled alive in 43-degree temperatures and traipsed through the gardens of Seville with a coterie of Americans we had met, looking at Renaissance cathedrals and sipping ice-cold cokes and Calippo ices.

We spent days in Paris, looking at the sights and feeling sophisticated. We ate out at night with the Eiffel tower in the background, having baguettes with soft goat's cheese on the grass. We lost ourselves in the Louvre and took turns snapping photos of ourselves in front of the Mona Lisa. We bumped into a TV commercial being filmed in a main street not so far from the Arc de Triomphe and spent an age watching actors flit in and out of shot.

We noticed the things about the French capital that differed from London or the US, the shapes of phone booths and post boxes. We marvelled with glee at the funny women with little dogs we had heard so about. But all good things come to an end, and my mate and I left Paris at Gare de Nord where Grand TGVs waited to head to destinations like Montpelier, St Raphael and Toulon.

Rachael and I have corresponded by letter, me in my little

writing which takes a lot of effort, and her in bubble-writing, like a fifth-form schoolgirl.

# 6 MAKING HEADWAY

*The wind and the waves are always on the side of the ablest navigators.* Edmund Gibbon

Before I fell asleep, I had knocked my head seven times on the pillow so as to wake at 7 am. Superstition? It works, and my eyes flutter open just before the second hand of my Citizen sports watch reaches two minutes before the hour. I am used to being away, and it doesn't take me long to realise where I am.

I squeeze out of the tight space, bare feet on the floor. I slip past the sleeping crew up through the companionway, up top, to see a cracker of a morning. There's a chill in the March air, and a breeze sends ripples through the water of the marina. The tree line of the surrounding countryside starts at the water's edge, save for where a road meanders, and these woods stack up the hillside in thickets that go for miles. Birds flutter from tree to tree, chirping and singing.

At this time of year, we are past the vernal equinox, but the sun is still to make an emphatic appearance. The forecast assures us it will, though, and that the prevailing breeze will stay constant. Perfect.

James appears in the cockpit and fetches a tobacco tin and paper from inside his fleece, yawning and breaking wind conspiratorially.

"Morning," I greet him.

He nods. We make small talk—I imagine with a mental grin we look like a Second World War U-boat captain and his second-in-command. I shiver, involuntarily, in my t-shirt and shorts, and note I'm going to need my fleece. I'm also gagging for a coffee but there's only instant here—I checked last night.

I drop down and peer around, getting a fresh perspective of our new home. There's the chart table with a map lying on it. Behind the companionway, a nook on both sides, where two people can sleep in the stern—James, as skipper, takes one quarter berth—and Garry has taken the other. Garry has left his bright jacket over a chair, ready for the day. I spot a radio on the table past the bulkhead. A door to the bathroom turns out to hide a shower compartment as well. A cushioned bench runs either side of the table with space along the hull for someone to sleep—Mark is rubbing his eyes and stretching out in his bag, yawning.

Claire twists and sits up in her space at the bow.

"How did everyone sleep?" she asks, to break the silence.

"Like a baby," I reply.

She smiles and rummages in the backpack at her feet.

James joins us and stands at the ladder. He sees me looking at all the gizmos and says:

"Steve, as you can see, we have Radar, GPS, Navtex, VHF radio —all the standard navigational instruments."

*Great. No chance of getting lost here.*

"We can cook, there's a pressurised water system and shower,"—he points at the bathroom door. He pries open a door with this knee—"a refrigerator," pulls open a drawer—"and even cutlery and crockery."

I fill a kettle, set it down on the gas ring, and spoon a few heaps of Nescafe into a spare mug. Mark and Eric join me at the table, elbows propped on top. Claire pins up her hair, puts on a baseball cap, and perches, cross-legged on the bunk. Breakfast is cereal served out of Tupperware boxes into modest, acrylic 1970s bowls.

"The breakfast of champions," Eric says, cracking his knuckles, making us grimace.

We eat steadily, and politely, considerate of the fact we don't know each other well yet. It's all I can manage not to upturn my bowl and sink the sugary milk at the bottom. James and Eric, the old sweats, discuss tides—we are on a rising tide which will probably mean more to the local fisherman on the jetties. They'll be looking for channels where they can find fish.

James stands up and puts his cap on and looks like he is ready to get things moving.

"Where to Skipper?" asks Garry, taking the hint, and he glances at the map.

Unfurling it, fold by fold, James stabs a finger at a spot, and we peer over his arm.

"Rothesay," he says, confirming our destination. "That's across the Clyde on the other side to the west. It's technically part of the Highlands."

It's not that far, squinting at the map. Looking at Glasgow, there's a sort of a large leaf-like feature that hangs off the Scottish coast as James clarified. Part of this landscape is an island—Bute Island. Rothesay is sited on its eastern edge. It's a fishing stop easily reached in a day, so is the obvious place to head for.

I glance at my watch and stand. We have plenty of time to get there. Sunset is past 8 pm, and we have Daylight Saving, so we can take advantage of the lengthening days.

We zipper up our fleeces, grab lifejackets, and muster on deck.

"Let's do it crew," Claire says from the vantage point of the cockpit, arm on the railing, ready to depart like a soldier on the Normandy beaches in 1944.

Eric and Mark, used to working together, spring into action and untie our mooring ropes from the bollards and stop us drifting by leaving a turn around to take the strain.

James turns a key, and the small engine roars to life.

"Okay, let's get going," he announces.

Eric and Mark push off together, leaping back on board at the front and rear, and we drift off, rocking in the swell that bounces off the jetty wall. James opens the throttle, and we pull safely away, the bow pointing into the marina.

For this first leg, James will skipper and allocate roles. The instruction is "monkey-see-monkey-do" and as the others have more experience than me, I watch, hoping I can assist until I find my sea legs.

The air is still crisp, and thankfully, there is the hint of a breeze as we motor out into deeper waters using the "donkey", the old mariner's word for an engine. Engines are considered rather *gauche* by sailors, noisy and smoky, and why would you guzzle fuel when you can get by with nothing but the elements? We pass fishing vessels with nets, men and women sorting tackle, boats that have overnighted and are on their way back to port. I notice a rust-specked speed limit affixed to the wharf:

*10 mph*

This is not the time to race. Once we are past the harbour, James takes a swig of water from a bottle and hands the wheel to Eric. He's pleased to be given an early appointment and takes *Heavenly* out towards the Clyde on a heading James shows him on the chart.

*Heavenly* enters the firth and without the protection of the breakwaters, we wallow side to side longitudinally in the chop. We're not sailing yet, but we are *under way*. There's the occasional speckle of spray from the water and I finger my zip. The breeze picks up.

The sun makes a welcome appearance from behind the cumulus clouds, and Eric fishes a pair of flash Ray-Bans out of his Musto jacket.

I listen to Garry as he talks to James about the design of *Heavenly*: it makes little sense to me.

"She's got a fin with rudder on skeg," James says. Garry nods.

When I ask, this means *Heavenly* has a fin to help her glide through the water's currents. It turns out some boats have deeper keels than others. Some designs allow the boat to be stable, good for ocean crossings, others might have speed in mind.

Once *Heavenly* is out in open waters, it's clear it's time for the business of sailing.

*Let's hoist the sails.*

I look upwards—*Heavenly* has a mainsail and headsail

configuration. This means we have sails "fore" and "aft", front and back. We hoist the triangular sail by a halyard attached to the masthead.

The mainsail, literally the main sail, is wrapped along the boom, the large metal pole which extends from the mast and reaches out towards us. I've heard these can swing suddenly and whack the unsuspecting sailor.

*I'll be careful.*

Claire helps Eric take the sail cover off, and into a storage locker where it's kept. They wrestle the foresails out of the lockers.

"Hook that foresail on to the forestay at the base," James says. "That's right," he encourages.

The foresail is hauled up under the guidance of Eric and Garry.

"Let's raise the mainsail," James says.

It's all I can do not to add "My hearties," but this won't help.

Glad to be doing something physical, I grab part of the halyard and pull when everyone else does, but we are out of sync.

"One–two–heave!" I call, hoping people will take my lead. They do.

"Two–six," I switch into the term I've heard the Royal Marines use, which sounds legitimate.

The sail ascends the mast, furl by furl. Claire takes in the slack, levering away on a winch.

"Yup–take it up to the masthead," James says, "all the way now, and you're done."

He looks happy and takes another swig of water.

# 7 A POINT OF DIFFERENCE

From watching TV, as far as I can tell, sailing life seems to be people in waterproofs huddled over winches winding frantically, but our progress is at a much more pedestrian and leisurely pace. Minutes tick by, and we leave the marina well behind, until it is just a speck.

*Heavenly* speeds up, and we can sense its passage through the waters of the Clyde, birds circling above and flitting past the mast, mouths open and calling. Eric wears a pleased expression, and Garry is clearly in his element.

I glance around at my crew mates.

*They all look competent.*

It hits me with a sinking feeling. I'm the only one with no experience. James stands in the cockpit, glancing up at the sails and peering at us. Claire appears capable, and scurries around helping. Mark strikes me as the sort of person who only asks questions the answer to which they already know.

*Heavenly* is cruising nicely, canted over to the port side with the keel ploughing through the water, birds still wheeling overhead.

*Which side is port*? I ask myself, racking my brains. It's the left side, I remember. People have taught me helpful lines like "the Captain LEFT his PORT behind," or "Stars are bright and so is RIGHT".

It goes without saying, learning the lingo and the ropes, literally, is all part of the experience.

The breeze strengthens, in our favour, perhaps to a Force Four —a "Moderate Breeze". This is nothing to be alarmed about. It's a lovely wind to make headway in, and we definitely don't want to be becalmed, stuck out here. The sail canvas is tensioned to take advantage as Mark, sunglasses on in the sunshine, takes a wind on the winch—he looks a pro. James nods appreciatively as this happens without his beckoning.

I notice the wind is in our faces: it seems a miracle *Heavenly* can sail forward against it, which is counter-intuitive to me. I ask Claire.

"We're close-hauled," she says, "we are beating into the wind."

This still makes little sense.

Surely, that's not how it works? I also notice we are sailing towards the shore—could we do with heading a bit more the other way? James calls out at just the right volume to be heard:

"Ready about!"

All of a sudden: a hive of activity as Claire rushes to stand by the mainsheet to manage the main sail. Mark slides up front by the foresail, or gib. What is going on? She reads the look on my face.

"We're tacking," she announces, smiling.

We're changing direction—"coming about" as it's called—heading back across the channel, still heading west. The wind was streaming from the port quarter. Now it will be from the starboard quarter, a full 90 degrees.

"I was beating south of south-west for 3 hours."

"I was running at 10 knots with a following sea."

If you ever catch the sailing at the Summer Games on the TV or overhear two old salty men in polo shirts with their collars turned up talking about it, you will hear them use those words like "close-hauled."

*How does sailing actually work?*

It makes sense that the wind pushes you from behind. That's known as running, on a "following sea"—the wind is pushing the wave tops to you.

If it's coming from the side, you are on a "Broad Reach" or "Beam Reach", with your sail out to the sides.

*This makes sense, too.*

I turn to face James.

"How on earth do boats travel when the wind is heading

towards them, just like it is now?" I ask.

"Steve, I'll explain," Garry says, joining us.

"Sailors set their sails as close to the mast as they can, 'close hauled'. A curious effect allows them to sail forwards at about 45 degrees to the wind, or maybe closer. The sail acts like the wing of an aeroplane."

I nod.

"If you sail too near the wind though, you stop, and make no headway," Garry enlightens me.

"You've heard of the expression 'Sailing too close to the wind'!" James says.

"And, you'll likely be going the wrong way," Garry continues, as I had seen already.

"So, the trick is to keep turning to the other side of the wind. We will keep going in zig-zags."

He mimes this with his hand.

"And, each turn is known as a tack—you are, in other words, 'tacking' or 'beating' upwind. We'll get there eventually," Garry grins.

*I think I get it.*

Claire looks expectedly at James, and he calls out:

"Ready about!"

So, we go about: James whips the wheel over smartly, and as the bow comes around, the mainsail loosens off and eases as the wind drops out of it. It doesn't matter we get too close to the wind now. Our momentum will carry us to the other side.

The mainsail and boom come over, and Claire pulls on the sheets. I figure what is going on, and assist, taking up the slack. We secure them to a nearby cleat on deck. Mark and Eric sort the foresail out next: as it flaps and loses air, they pull it through to the other side, and secure it likewise.

"Steve." James comes and stands next to me, rubbing his hands together.

"So–that's tacking. If the wind was behind us, and we had to change course, we'd move the stern through the wind. That's called gybing. We'll do that tomorrow."

Contemplating this, the sun meanders higher, and we feel warmer for the first time. Those of us who have put on too many layers ditch lifejackets and divest a layer.

James reinforces the point:

"These directions we are going in, relative to the wind direction, are known as 'points of sail'."

I nod appreciatively.

"Don't worry, it will become clearer tomorrow."

Later, I draw them in my notebook:

REACH  RUNNING  TACKING

So, having been schooled in the basics, we turn our attention to our progress towards our next port. Rothesay will appear as a smudge on the far shore, through the haze. We crane to the horizon to see if we can spot the town, or the 13th century ruined castle.

"Another hour, crew, and we will be there," warns James.

As we approach shore from the east, the wind shifts. We make an adjustment, and our mainsail is now pointing to the side.

"We're on a broad reach, now," Eric says.

The shore looms closer and closer, the houses and roads showing as boxes and lines, resolving into houses that resemble Lego, the roads silver ribbons; then a real town with a church spire comes into focus. Low-lying mist obscures the hills behind the town. The chatter tails off, and everyone is quiet.

We glide up to the long arm of the jetty, and James indicates the berth we will tie up at.

ROTHESAY

## 8 IT'S A BUTE FIRST NIGHT IN ROTHESAY

We drift towards the unoccupied berth, relieved the first day is over. The concentration has wearied us, and the fresh air has taken its toll. Even the old sweats look tired, as they've been at their desks for weeks.

I check our surroundings.

There's a clock tower poking out from a tawny-red roof with miniature turrets at the corners. Well-cut grass abuts the harbour, where locals stroll for a spring evening, with the lure of summer approaching. Terraced houses with attic rooms perched up top stand proudly with prestige cars out front. And a collection of what, surely, would have been workers' cottages, crafted from local stone and hewn wood.

James watches us glide *Heavenly* at a pedestrian pace up to the mooring point with our fenders overboard, to take the impact, and I jump out carefully, as I don't want to land in the water, or be sandwiched between boat and pier. In the distance, I spot The Victoria Hospital, which I understand has an Accident & Emergency unit and I don't need to be the one from the course to end up in it. I grab a painter and take a turn around the bollard until Garry can show me the clever knot I require.

There's little encouragement needed, and time enough for a brisk walk over to the local pub. James leads through the door and we gather at the bar, waiting for the barmaid to get to us.

"What can I get you?" she says.

We stand in a corner with our drinks, our skin reddening and smarting from the breeze, feeling sleepy. The sun descends below cloud cover, its rays casting low through the windows into our eyes, and we turn around so we can still see to talk about the day. Locals listen to our out-of-town accents, and I suspect, think little of the English blow-ins with their city ways, while James acknowledges people who recognise him with a nod and a greeting.

Garry regales us about his crewing life to date. He has been to Australia and the Med, as well as up here.

"Yup, I reckon the Clyde and waterways are amongst the best cruising in Western Europe," affirms James.

"I have spent years in these waters and have come back time and time again to my favourite spots. Look at the chart. There are hundreds of spots. Why head to the South of France when there's excellent cruising much closer here?"

I can see a bunch of nodding heads as everyone digests this, and no one disagrees.

Back at the boat, as it's getting dark, James looks at me and his face takes on a more irritated look for once, rather than the usual patient instructor one he normally wears. He glances down at my feet.

"What are those trainers you are wearing, Steve?"

"Nikes, James," I reply.

They are half-decent Nike Airs with a bubble enclosed in the heel—all the rage—with a black rubber sole. Whilst they are fit for purpose and prevent me from sliding overboard and out of sight, they are also leaving marks on the fiberglass deck, so I'm dispatched with a damp cloth to remove them. I carry out this task dutifully but cursing myself for my naivety and for mucking up a fine boat. It's the only time James picks me up on a point this week.

Things improve: settled in for the evening on the couches around the table, we're offered a nip of single malt whisky from a collection James keeps in stock, in a corner locker, pride of place. I can't pretend to be a connoisseur, but with gentle encouragement from my elders, I accept. The amber liquid Glenlivet assaults my tongue and numbs the roof of my mouth and burns as I swallow.

James reaches for a packet of potato chips and tears them open and leaves them out enticingly. He holds forth and talks about his sailing off the Bay of Biscay, with Eric and Mark gazing at him studiously, listening carefully, looking at me briefly as I splutter on my whisky. He sees his opportunity to offer a refill.

"Steve, you want another one?"

"Yes, please, that first one was good."

Refusing to be beaten, I take another nip.

*This will put hairs on my chest.*

"We're off to Tarbert tomorrow," announces James after checking the forecast.

He places a finger of one hand at our current location, and traces a route across the chart on the table. That reminds me of a question I had this first day.

"How do we know where we are, at sea?" I ask James.

"We do have a GPS on board," he says, pointing out a grey box with LCD display with plastic buttons and dials.

There's a rubberized antenna sitting proudly on top. The technology is still new. Armoured regiments used them in the Gulf war, and civilian hikers paid a premium for the sets you put in a pocket or a backpack, I remembered.

"How did you navigate before that, though?" I ask, "before the GPS satellites were launched?"

"Dead reckoning, Steve. Now–every sailor worth his salt knows this. It was on the syllabus at Dartmouth." He leans back in his chair and continues:

"When you knew your speed through the water, you could work out how far you had gone in a day. Ships' captains would use their ship's clock or timepiece to estimate this. It was of course inaccurate, and after weeks at sea, vessels would be out by literally hundreds of nautical miles."

"What's a nautical mile?" I ask, taking the risk of looking a fool.

There's no such thing as a stupid question, I remember, then correct myself: maybe there is.

"It's a bit more than a mile." James is always patient.

"But you have to take into account the tide and sea currents, it's not an exact science," he continues.

As modern travellers, we are blessed with accurate timekeeping, not using a ship's clock, but by the quartz watches on our wrists. What's more, we have the luxury of tuning in to BBC *Radio Four* if we reckon our watches are out at the start of a trip.

Later, before I fall asleep, I twist and turn in my sleeping bag and my thoughts drift to Rachael. I wonder what she is up to. Possibly watching TV with a glass of wine, thinking about her horses. She would be getting up in six hours to muck them out, I figure, not wanting to switch places with her right now. We will both be up to cool mornings, but the forecast suggests the weather will hold, and remain dry here.

# 9 ARGYLL HIGHLANDERS

On the program today—a venture to a port called Tarbert. So, from the Isle of Bute, along the coast of the leaf-shaped shore, from right to left.

"We'll follow the coastline clockwise to the west," comments James.

Tarbert guards access to the Mull of Kintyre and the Inner Hebrides. The Mull is the huge peninsular of land that hangs out from the Scottish coast here. The town sits on the east side, half-way down, on an isthmus, or neck of land, only a mile long, that separates waters both sides of the peninsula. It's home to a thousand people.

The Mull of Kintyre. It's not only a song by Paul McCartney. It's also described by some, mischievously, as a male-shaped appendage, that protrudes, poking towards Ireland.

"It's a bit rude," Mark says, with a wicked look of glee on his face. "It's even become the yardstick for obscenity in film, would you believe—'the angle of the dangle'."

We nod, who knew that?

We will head out into the waters, then strike out for the safety of the land again by nightfall. It's sort of a hop, a leap of faith. And if you excuse the analogy, we are heading for the underside of the male appendage, where it comes out of the groin.

Our passage will see us leave the Island of Arran well to our south. This substantial and famous isle provides a reassuring back stop, and a big shelter from the more open waters of the Irish sea which finish at the bluffs of the Northern Ireland coast.

"If you were to run south-west the other way, you'd end up at Belfast," James says, enjoying the geography lesson.

Placing my finger on the scale, I can see Arran is about 30 miles long, not much smaller than the Isle of Man further south. My take: that's enough to keep you occupied for a weekend or two.

We are away in good time, shivering into our jackets as the breeze gusts suddenly. As we get into open waters, we spy the ferry from Wemyss Bay steaming across our track. The bay is on the Scottish mainland, accessible from Glasgow by road. Our mode of transport will be by boat though—*we chose to sail.* Mark fusses around, tightening a sheet here, craning up every so often, looking at his father.

I still don't get whether we are sailing well, especially when we are beating into the wind, close-hauled.

"How can we ensure we're making good headway?" I ask.

Eric points up and says:

"See those little strips of tape streaming from the sail near the mast?"

I look up and can see them all pointing downwind behind us.

"Yup."

"Tell-tails," Eric says. "They should be out straight, mate–that tells you how much wind you've got. As you get close to the wind, turn the wheel until they are going full pelt."

"So, if they ease off, then I know I am too close?" I ask.

"You've got it, Steve. You'll need to bring her back then, with the wheel."

"Got it," I repeat.

As we get within sight of Tarbert, we spot the narrow isthmus of land. I can see farmhouses and dwellings just in sight. Claire points out a farmer in a patchwork field with his dog, and a tractor at the tilled edge.

*The isthmus.*

What a word. In the 18th century, sea-going vessels were being hauled over the neck to avoid the dangers of storms and tidal races in the seas surrounding the Mull of Kintyre. The town name is the anglicised Gaelic word *tairbeart*, which means "carrying across".

"Yup, they would have been able to carry small boats over that land," James says.

Case in point, he explains. In the 11<sup>th</sup> century, the King of Norway had his ship carried across to lay claim to the town. The peace treaty he signed said that any land he could sail was his. Robert the Bruce did it too, during the Scottish Wars of Independence.

The port is of course, in a sheltered cove, where else? As we cruise through the headland past a humped island topped with heather, the wind drops, and the waters assume the surface of a millpond.

*No need to hang on so tight.*

The tide is low, and a muddy rock shoal is exposed, flecked with seaweed. The masts of boats stand proudly, perpendicular to the shoreline. Our eyes are drawn to the church tower.

We can see a ruined castle in the lee of a crest, protecting the harbour entrance, surrounded by grass and heath, the occasional wildflower dotted around, left to run amok. There's an air of desolation. Moss and lichen run across the top of the old stone, and a Saint Andrew's Cross Scottish flag flies from a pole, drooping down for now in the still air. Also, a flat pitch of land—space for a ball game perhaps, with a wooden seat for a spectator.

A pub with an upper storey in yellow is stark, compared to the buildings next to it, but competes with a house gaily painted cyan next to it. *Sponsored by Dulux?*

We have two options: either a marina to the north, or a mooring area right next to the road. The ship's company are unanimous in preferring the second option as it's closer to the pub.

James asks us if we would like to eat out again for the evening. He gets a resounding sea of nods from the group, and everyone reaches for a pocket, anticipating a round of drinks.

The castle is accessible down a side street and a quick cut across heathland. I ask Claire if she wants to go and look, sort of in *Famous Five* fashion. She puts on her trainers, and we head up the laneway, which peters out to short grass leading up. It's easy going through the wildflowers, and it's trivial avoiding rocks that are scattered in the field on the way up.

The old keep has a little veranda accessed by steps, and an open door topped with a wooden lintel into the paved ground floor. We peer into the depths. The area is tiny, barely fifteen metres across. There's a damp, empty, window where water has trickled down from the roof.

We look down on to the humped island, and then at the boats, and see James lighting his pipe in the distance. He spots us silhouetted above him and raises an arm in acknowledgement of our achievement.

"Let's head down," Claire says.

I follow her as she jogs off back, her trainers getting soaked as her feet sink into the grass.

We spy Eric and Mark crossing the pub threshold, and we quicken the pace to join them. Re-united in the saloon, we appreciate its warmth with a real fire lit to ward off the chill of the evening this far north.

"What are the specials?" asks Garry, craning up at the board.

"Soup of the Day–Mushroom. Local catch with chips, Roast Beef," reads Mark out loud.

*I'm hungry. I could eat a horse, then chase the jockey.*

I'm pleased to see a choice of steak on the menu with porterhouse on special. Mine arrives drenched with a mushroom sauce, cut in half with a soft, rare interior surrounded by a seared crust. It goes down well with a pint of Guinness, and there is a glorious sticky date pudding to finish with.

And later, I wonder if I can get to a phone box to call Rachael.

## TARBART

## 10 MICHAEL, ROW THE BOAT ASHORE

James joins me and Claire on top for an instant Nescafe in the morning. It's cold again in harbour, and when it was light, I walked briefly to the local newspaper shop for the paper whilst everyone slept, also a chance to get a better first coffee and a packet of chocolate biscuits. It's a stolen moment away from the confined space onboard. Eric appreciates the *Daily Express* I got him, and busies himself with the business section.

"Where to today, Skipper?" I ask James.

"See how we're on the side of a huge inlet or waterway?" he replies.

I nod.

"We'll continue up that loch today, Loch Fyne."

We now plan to trawl north up this loch, which, while substantial at the southern end, over two miles across at the firth mouth, tapers to maybe a mile as it heads north.

"...and further up, we're heading to Lochgair," James says.

Lochgair (Gaelic: *An Loch Geàrr*) is a village. It lies on Loch Gair, a small, classically formed horseshoe shaped cove on the west side. This will protect us tonight should the wind pick up.

"Have you read any of Iain Bank's books?" Garry says, looking up suddenly.

"No," I reply.

"That village is the main setting in his 1992 book *The Crow Road*, he replies.

"Have you read it?" I ask.

"No, but I will now," he retorts with a grin.

This will mark the northerly limit of our voyage this week.

The inlet is well up the guts of the countryside: the intrepid traveller who journeys to the end as far as they can is not far off well-known and larger Loch Lomond, cross-country. As we trawl the coast, we keep one eye on the closer west shore, and another out for anything we can spot on the eastern side. I spot a single, white, exposed house enjoying water views and access. The people who live here do so in splendid isolation. It also reminds me of the tourist spots you see in the English Lake District right out of *Swallows and Amazons*.

Low-lying mist which has threatened to deposit drizzle on us all day, making Claire shake with cold, clears, and the spring sun shines, then beats out of a sky which comes bluer and more iridescent by the half-hour. The improving weather has transformed the relative menacing air of the water into a more idyllic spot—proof weather can make or break your safety. If we felt a sense of foreboding, we can now replace it with a sense of ease.

The cove is a great chance to learn how to use our anchor, and overnight aboard, relatively untouched by the tide and any worsening weather. We spend an hour trawling through the cove laying it. James wants us all to have a go at letting out the anchor and how it feels when it holds on the seabed, showing us how much the rope unwinds as the anchor burrows, and finally catches.

There's an option to use a second anchor to secure us in our spot.

"But today, we will make do with one, and you'll see we will naturally drift around during the night," James says.

"Okay, let's row to the shore and back. Steve–your chance to have a go in the dinghy," James says. "Then I can sign you off as competent."

*Great.*

He lowers the boat down and we get in.

"Come down too, Claire," he calls. "let's get the boat loaded up for Steve."

She turns to face *Heavenly* and climbs down whilst we hold still: the boat sits lower in the water.

"Okay, I'm sure you can work it out–off you go," James says.

I grasp both oars in a firm grip, and with small strokes start towards the shore. I make sure my oars are in the water before pulling back evenly, I don't want to be "catching crabs" and ending up on my back. I remember my father rowing my brother and I across the local duck pond in Ruislip, north-west London, when I was a boy. He made it seem easy.

"That's the way," James comments.

When we get to the shore, we decide to have a look up and down it before heading back, seeing as we've made it this far. There's a car for sale on the foreshore, an old Vauxhall Cavalier—asking price 1,500 pounds. It's got bald tyres, I notice.

I also spot a telephone box which reminds me to check if I've got a signal on my mobile, so I fish it out of the inner pocket of my fleece where I've placed it in a freezer bag to keep dry. No signal at all, so I grab the door handle, smoothed out by thousands of hands. There's the smell of urine and mustiness from phone directories housed in a metal shelf. The receiver is prehistoric Bakelite, but I spot the crown and EIIR (Elizabeth the Second Regina) stamped above the door. I dial Rachael's number and she answers after a few rings.

"Rachael. It's Steve."

"How's the sailing?" she replies.

"Good. What are you up to?" I ask.

There's a brief silence.

"Watching tv, nothing on, though." She pauses. "Any pretty girls on board?" she adds playfully.

"Just the one girl our age," I say, not really answering the question.

"Okay, cool," she replies.

"She's a medical student," I tell her.

"Bet she's clever then."

"Probably," I say, leaving it at that for now.

Looking through the glass door, I can see James waiting, wanting to call Jane, so I wind up the conversation:

"See you when I get back to England, right?"

He holds the door open for me and we switch places, and he presses fifty-pence pieces into the coin slot.

Claire is standing by the dinghy waiting for us. We row back to *Heavenly* and climb back up inside as darkness falls, and an owl hoots from the shore. We are pleased not to have to tie up to a pier or jetty and welcome the calm, up and down motion drift of *Heavenly* at anchor.

Claire admits she is dying for a shower, even a cold one, so James offers she can take one in the toilet or 'heads', that ancient Royal Navy term—the little compartment opposite the ladder.

"Thanks James, I hate being mucky," she says.

She disappears for fifteen minutes and is back in ten, shivering, wearing a clean change of clothes.

"That water is *cold*, James," she says in a low tone, not wanting to come over as a whinger. "And—I cracked my head on the sill as I was getting out, I was that fast."

"In summer, you all could have had solar showers," James says. We've got a bag that we can hoist up the mast, Claire. You get a few minutes of water in which to rinse."

He rummages in the first aid kit and gets her a band aid.

"There you go, that will sort you. And I suggest you join us in another tipple. Look, I've got another bottle for you and Steve to try."

He looks in the locker above his head over the chart table—his captain's secret supply.

"You got a secret stash there, Skipper?" I ask.

James smiles enigmatically.

# LOCH GAIR

## 11 GOING DEEPER

Sure enough, in the morning, when I pop my head up, I can see we have drifted slowly in a circle in the night, and where the east shore was visible from the companionway, now the west shore is in view. A house built from grey stone sits opposite us, smoke billowing from a chimney. We spot a chicken coop, and a cow, and I bet there are pigs in the outhouse too, so Mark muses there's the possibility of a cooked breakfast fit for the apocryphal king at this hour. There's a temptation to go over, knock on the door and invite ourselves in.

"So, we drifted, but we are still quite secure," remarks James, inspecting our anchor when he comes up top to join us. "We haven't moved off—*Heavenly* is still *on*."

We've come as far as we've planned on the course, so will now backtrack to Rhu marina. We will take a more southerly course and will make stops elsewhere, rather than retrace our exact steps to Rothesay, where we spent the first night.

Time now, though, to head back via Tarbert.

There is plenty of time and a good wind behind us, so we don't rush in getting away, and luxuriate over a breakfast of bacon and eggs sandwiches. James chases bacon around a pan, sending sizzling fumes throughout the cabin. He must have heard us talking. He reaches up and unpegs the cabin window to let the steam escape.

We spend the morning cruising up and down the loch, practising coming about, bow or stern first. We hope to complete the final miles quickly, as our stomachs rumble and appetites are building by the afternoon. It's colder, as the wind gusts, and we shelter in the cockpit. As we've done the route in reverse, we are familiar with it, so the leg goes by quickly. Boats come by in the opposite direction, and we pass them, port side to port side, heading starboard (right) to avoid a collision. There are rules of the road, in fact. In general, power boats give way to sail with a few exceptions.

I am getting the hang of sailing. It's all slotting in, and making sense—watching and waiting, and paying attention paid off. I'm at the wheel when we need to change course with the wind behind us. We need to turn the stern of *Heavenly* through the wind—and I call out the command for this:

"Bearing away!"

As the boom comes over quickly, James yells:

"Gybe-O!"

On a small sailing boat, we would all duck in unison. Nobody wants to be the one unlucky enough to get hit. It might look dangerous, but it's also more efficient than tacking we did on the first day. There is no point in the turn where there is no wind.

"It's also possible to gybe accidentally when the wind changes and the boom comes over on its own without warning," Mark says. "Watch out for that."

*I will, sounds dangerous.*

"We can add a 'preventer' to tie the boom to the deck so that doesn't happen, but we have to keep an eye on it," he adds.

"Look, we can secure the boom to two points, port and starboard, and let off the correct side off to gybe the boat as the stern comes around."

*Expert advice.*

There's a hint of gloom, and the light is fading by the time we approach Tarbert and spy the castle again, and the sky changes colour as we motor up to the harbour wall. There's an old bloke —a sea dog—with a worn Captain's Birdseye cap standing on the jetty watching us when we round the corner. He's got a pipe and a large packet of tobacco, which he clasps as if it's his lotto ticket.

Us young 'uns make a quick sortie to the local supermarket before it closes to get milk for our tea and coffee, and we carefully board using the deck lights to find Eric and Garry playing cards. All hands onboard agree we can call it a night early, and Mark gets out a book and reclines on his bunk. Later, as I mull over the trip so far, the ship's company is sound asleep tucked in early—the whisky accounted for and back in the cupboard. Both Garry and Eric are snoring. Claire turns over several times but doesn't wake, then falls into a deep sleep.

*** 

I can hear a light drizzle when I awake. The others are up already talking quietly in the cabin, hands in pockets, waiting for the kettle to boil. If there was a reluctance to get up on top, this would be the time.

We've enjoyed night stopovers in towns and pubs, but Kames will be a quieter stop. It's a hamlet on the Cowal peninsula, on the west arm of the Kyles of Bute. Inspecting the map, I can see it's the *left* edge of the large, dappled "leaf on the tree branch" I noted before. I steer *Heavenly* at times for this leg, gaining confidence at the wheel and James thinks I am picking it up nicely.

When we arrive, the foreshore is straight, and we see a well-tended, manicured lawn running along a small strip of pebbled beach. There's a Victorian era cast iron metal railing which divides the grass from the beach, the sort of metal that would take your teeth out if you slipped on it.

Upturned dinghies lie on the shingle, out of action for the time being, owners nowhere to be seen. People don't just make off with stuff around here by the looks of it.

Hills abound to the extremities, and peaks over our shoulder have a rugged look to them, low-lying, but with the promise of danger in bad weather. Low cloud hovers over them, the possibility of a squall to come.

Once again, we take to the table in the cabin, sitting around it with our shoes off, sleeves rolled up. Claire sits cross-legged on her bunk and James perches by the chart. The whisky bottle comes out again, and we break open four-packs of beers. We exchange stories about Scotland and destinations across the globe.

*Pull up a sandbag—swing the lantern.*

Eric tells us of some of the places crewing has taken him throughout the world. He's been down the coast of France to Spain, across the Bay of Biscay and out to places like Cyprus in the Mediterranean. He is aiming for the "Yachtmaster" certificate, which is the whole kit and kaboodle and the pinnacle for blue water sailing and crewing.

There are other certificates keen sailing types can earn—a bit like me collecting my childhood swimming badges. I've heard of "Tidal Coastal Skipper", which is about sticking safely to the littorals of coasts before attempting to head across a sea. But I'm more interested in trans-ocean sailing. I take my chance.

"What's 'Blue Water' sailing?" I ask.

I know the answer, but want to steer the conversation over to the big topics.

"It's open sea cruising, and ocean crossings," replies Eric.

What we've been doing is green water sailing which is coastal —with the shore in sight most of the time. I know enough about blue water sailing to understand that you have to be competent. Stories of sailors who have got into difficulties out in the Pacific are two-a-penny.

"How big a boat do you need to cross an ocean like the Atlantic?" I ask him.

"30 foot should do it, I reckon Steve," he replies. *"Heavenly* would manage it."

He continues, "The thing is, though, the Pacific is rougher–it's less protected. And people who cross the tropics are not exactly heading into the roaring forties, furious fifties or screaming sixties down south."

He's right—as a vessel navigates Cape Horn, at the base of the South American continent, it braves the treacherous waters of the Southern Ocean. Many a ship has come to grief down there. The Suez Canal opened in the 19$^{th}$ century, an engineering feat that took years to complete. The Panama Canal, in Central America, opened in the 20$^{th}$. Both solved the age-old problem of going the "long way" around.

KAMES

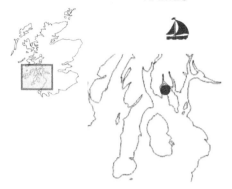

## 12 FAIR ISLES

One more night away. A chance to layover at Millport, on Cambrae Island, which we left well to the south on the way out. The final stop before we head back to the marina.

We can afford to bask in sunshine on the cruise over there, and we strip down to t-shirts, enjoying the warmth, and the clear views to the shoreline as the miles pass by. Claire tells me about her medical course, and the hands-on experience she is getting on wards. It seems fascinating, I can barely find a pulse during first-aid sessions.

Mark goes below for a while to look at the engine compartment with his father. I can spot him through the roof cabin light, which is screwed tightly down to prevent spray from entering. Seeing me peering down, he makes faces, and we laugh.

Millport's an unassuming town on the south side of the island. The island sits to the south-east opposite our leaf-like feature we have got to know. Approaching port, we find a passage down towards the harbour, and we chug along under the engine. We discover a pretty horseshoe bay overlooked by two-storey buildings at the end—we can recognise a sort of an English south-west coast-Riviera vibe.

There is a sandy beach running along the road, with an iron rail fence. I can picture Edwardian ladies and gentlemen inching gently into the water, the ladies in bloomers, and the men—trousers rolled up and a hat against the benign July Scottish sun.

Between rock islands, there's a little reef. Here the water is surprisingly clear, almost aquamarine, in the slanting light this late in the afternoon.

"I imagine the water supports a fair amount of biodiversity," says our scientist, Claire.

The bay is also enlivened by a crocodile someone has painted on a rock that breaks the water. An artist has fashioned jaws out of metal, and painted a gum line, and added eyes.

Looking inland, I can see water meadows. To my eye, they resemble the water meadows in Salisbury, Wiltshire, several hundred miles to the south.

The obvious place to moor for the night is a small concrete pier that rakes gingerly out into the bay. I see an entrance to a dock, with a stone slipway to the road. Pier or dock? The dock is perhaps more protected. I glance at James expectantly.

"First come, first served, no need to book," observes James. "Good weather expected, let's just tie up at the pier," he gestures.

We motor up to our mooring point. We stand against the side of the boat, shins lined up, knees locked out. Garry has a mooring rope in hand, waiting.

"Ready," shouts James from his place in the cockpit.

*We can do the work now. He can remain seated.*

James cuts the engine as we approach. Mark points *Heavenly* carefully as she glides to the pier. We've thrown the mooring fenders overboard, and they take the impact like big barrage balloons. Garry leaps ashore and pulls hard on the painter, leaning back to draw us in. In the tug of war between a 75-kilogramme human, and a one-tonne boat, the human can win handsomely.

Eric is keen to point out Millport's tourist offerings: a tiny cathedral, and an equally tiny house.

"Yes, smallest extant cathedral in Europe," James reinforces.

*I must look up "extant".*

To ring the changes, we explore the waterfront. An older diesel car clatters past us, throwing water from a puddle over the pavement, narrowly drenching Claire. We hesitate at a street corner, then turn to explore a few blocks away from the shore. It's a good chance to scout out the hostelries. We select a likely candidate.

"Pre-dinner drink?" Eric stops in a pub door. "To whet the appetite?"

To settle any dispute, he enters before we can answer.

I join my elders and agree to a cheeky gin and tonic. We then retire to *Heavenly* for supper. Mark leads off at a cracking pace, and we follow, retracing our steps. He discovers he has a blister, and we stop at a bench overlooking the sea, with a lone seagull crying on a bollard, whilst we wait for him to rearrange a sock.

Dinner is cooked by the ever-obliging James and a duty skivvy, who he nominates, with a barely concealed glee: Mark. This meal "living onboard" is pasta boiled in a large cast-iron saucepan with a sauce from a bottle Mark is directed to, in a locker above the galley stove.

"Not that one, move along, no, too far. Yes, that one."

Mark scurries back and forth, unflustered.

We have an appetite from the day's work, and none of us are concerned about what we will eat even if we arrived as fussy eaters.

"You can always go hungry, no place to be a vegetarian or turn your nose up at anything," James says.

We nod. Fussy eaters hold their tongue. Mark dresses up the pasta with a simple Bolognaise sauce, and adds in mushrooms, carrots, and dried rosemary and basil from old spice pots he finds in the cupboards. He announces he has stirred the sauce enough and asks Claire to come forward.

"Have a taste, I need two people to check it out," he announces.

Claire and Eric pronounce the effort good enough, and relieved, Mark carries the pot to the table where we wait with bowls and forks, our stomachs rumbling. Eric's stomach growls. There is brief silence whilst we chew the first mouthfuls to satiate the appetite, then conversation once again.

Now's my chance to ask about the palm trees I have heard grow in Scotland. They grow on the Isle of Jura, in the Inner Hebrides. Nearby Craighouse is home to the Jura Distillery, James points out. And it gets warmer up on Lewis in the Outer Hebrides, in the Western Isles.

Speaking of whisky distilleries, time to pass around a different bottle: Claire doesn't seem too impressed by this offer, but she accepts a wee dram she can savour and hang on to. Eric leans in for a glass too, and smacks his lips after the first sip. This one is called Bowmore and has a far smokier taste than the Glenlivet we tried yesterday. I can't really decide between them. Whiskies in Scotland have signature tastes. The offerings from some of the Islay isles are smoky. I imagine bony workers bent over fires, rubbing smoke out of their eyes; others have a peaty taste. I imagine other workers floundering in the mud.

MILLPORT

# 13 DRILLS AND SKILLS

L ast day on board, last chances to impress, and we wake again to the metronomic rocking of *Heavenly* at its mooring. Breakfast is still cereal, but Garry whips up a bowl of rolled oats from an overlooked packet he has found in a cupboard and drizzles honey over the oats, licking the spoon.

Time to head back to Rhu, and there are important practical lessons for us to absorb, important last business to conduct. Once we've shaken off all the cobwebs, and have donned lifejackets, and grabbed our sunglasses and caps, we assemble up top. We are soon underway.

James calls for our attention:

"Man overboard drill," he announces, taking off his cap, roughing up his hair, and replacing it.

He grabs a spare lifejacket from the locker on top. With no preamble or explanation, he chucks it behind him, our eyes tracking its arc through the air into the water. This is literally immersion training for us—how will we react to this little crisis?

On trans-ocean voyages, falling over the side could mean certain death for any sailor, especially if he or she is travelling solo. Most solo sailors would as soon not be attached to the rail than stop breathing. There are stories of small boats being swamped by rogue waves in storms and rolling, mast down, before the buoyancy thrusts the boat back to the surface, righting it as she does. Sailors have been knocked momentarily unconscious only to wake, still tethered, but bruised and battered.

There is not much time to lose. Garry seems to know what to do, and, as he is at the wheel, he swings it hard over to port. The boat whips around, and we have the presence of mind to manage the boom as it comes over. The lifejacket has bobbed a fair distance already and James has his arm out pointing to it in the chop.

"30 metres, port side," he encourages.

Garry steers us to the jacket and as the straps scrape down the hull, James leans over with a hook, capturing it with a grunt.

"So that's the drill. Notice how fast our poor sailor drifted? We are doing"—he glances at the speed—"about four knots, and the current is with us–so he's vanishing faster than you think. We're lucky there's not much of a sea swell, and there's good vis out to where we last saw him."

He's right—if no one saw him fall, it could be over sooner than we'd like. And to ram home the lesson, James flings the lifejacket over the side again.

We repeat the drill and Mark recovers our "man over board" this time.

Next practical item on the agenda is rope tying. This is taught again in "monkey-see-monkey-do" fashion, and James delegates tuition to Eric, who takes us through the reef knot ("left over right, then under, right over left"), the bowline and clove hitch.

Luckily, I practised these in the cubs and scouts until I went blue with boredom, so can show some competence.

For the bowline—I mouth to myself.

*The rabbit comes out of the hole, around the tree—and back into the hole.*

I pass the end of the rope around the "tree", which is the "standing end", as I do.

James, seeing me finish first, ambles over to my bowline and pronounces it OK. He grabs the knot to ensure it's tidy—you never know, he might catch me out yet. It has to be "dressed" neatly to make sure it is secure.

Then I notice I've caught the sun on the back of my neck and my jacket collar is rubbing me sore—not much I can do now, but I hitch my t-shirt up a bit and wish I had packed the aloe vera.

***

On the way back into Rhu, we pass another island, another low-key and probably under-rated Scottish destination. As we come out of the lee shore—the sheltered side, a large boat drifts past our bow. It's not an elegant yacht like ours: it has a huge cabin, and a fiberglass superstructure monstrosity reaches into the sky above us, the top of the mast swinging like a pendulum. James snorts derisively and regards it down his nose.

"Just look at that gin palace," he exclaims, and shifts in his seat, glancing at Eric, barely concealing his disgust.

"Ay, she'd cost a packet," he replies.

Old-school sailors consider boats with engines to be vulgar, especially if they are not working boats, and full of slovenly revellers, like this one, even if the crew are professionals. As we pass to port, we look closer and see girls in bathing costumes, some with towels. It's on the cool side for sunbathing, but the sun is nonetheless making a guest appearance, and this is their chance to make a start on their summer tans.

Companions are pulling on warmer windcheaters and a few have a cigarette between lips or are passing packets and offering up lighters. The crew have poured drinks and distributed them amongst cheery guests.

We acknowledge the boat and her passengers with tidy hand waves, and the revellers raise a glass in our direction. One staggers and almost falls over, to a titter of laughter.

So, *Heavenly* returns to her home port at Rhu marina, voyage successful, crew all accounted for—no one lost in the waters on the Clyde. Jane is expecting us and is waiting in the Mondeo on the jetty with a thermos, a stack of cups, and a pack of sandwiches, a final token of stewardship. We exchange addresses and clap each other on the back. I thank Garry and Eric for their top tips and approach James. I thank him also for his time this week and wish him well.

"Send me a postcard. Next time I see you, you'll be a significantly more experienced sailor," James remarks.

I grin, and we shake on it.

# 14 CHARIOTS OF FIRE

I'm not going to head straight back to London. A friend of mine, Colin, is at Saint Andrews, on the other side of Scotland doing a postgrad, so I plan to break my trip and circle back that way to visit him on the way home. He picks me up at the train halt in windy Leuchars in a vintage Series Two Land Rover, similar to the one I saw Garry and Eric arrive in at Rhu marina.

"Looking good, Colin," I say.

"Loving the Landy, Steve," he gushes.

"Where did you get it from, mate?" I reply, admiring it.

"There's a sheep farmer near Loch Lomond who was getting rid of it. I offered him a thousand pounds, and he took it, didn't have to beat him down too far." He adds, "Did you bring your running kit, Steve?"

"I did," I reply.

He whizzes me around town, working through the gearbox, showing me the shops, the world-famous golf course, and points out some of his lecturers walking about. They parade in sports jackets with patches at the elbows, their collars turned up against the breeze. He is living out at an old farmhouse in Craighead, a little hamlet, and tells me we are going to meet up with his American girlfriend that he met on his course.

Before we meet her for dinner, Colin has to run an errand to the faculty to drop off a parcel. We go for a jog, and he leads out past the faculty. Classmates sit at a window with a cup of tea and wave, and I raise my hand in reply. We run down through the outskirts, and on to the foreshore, with the castle at one end. Colin angles for the sea and soon he is running through the water, flicking up spray from his feet. I prefer my line squelching along the sands, keeping my feet dry, but sinking in on every stride. Then I twig what he is up to: he's re-enacting the scene from the 1981 *Chariots of Fire* movie. Slick, but also amusing.

Abigail turns out to be petite with dark hair, an engaging, and personable girl from Maine who did her undergrad at Yale—an all-rounder and star. The pair seem suited to each other then, in fact, cutting a fun streak in this old college town on a different continent to her own. We race around the local countryside, and she draws parallels with New England. As she says, there are only two seasons over there, with Canada to the north and the north-easters coming in over the Atlantic,

"Two seasons, freezing and boiling hot," she notes with a wicked cackle.

We head into town to a large bar crammed full of well-heeled college folk—mostly Americans. A friend joins us, who drives an early model, but expensive looking, Mercedes. He is a quiet, but self-assured bloke from Vermont, wearing needle-point cord trousers and horn-rimmed spectacles, as collegiate and as fresh as the others at the table. It's altogether a pot of privilege and wealth, a far cry from diverse and grungier London.

I enjoy the wind-down on the train down south, opening a copy of Donna Tartt's *Secret History,* which was hanging around on the best-sellers charts. It's not my usual genre, but it flows decently enough, and I luxuriate in the prose, glad to be in one place for a few hours. The Intercity 225 plummets back down the East Coast Main Line, and I bury my head in the book, breaking off to grab a sandwich from the buffet car at Durham.

*\*\*\**

Content after my sailing sojourn, and a course pass, I arrive back in London clutching my brand-new sailing logbook with a flurry of entries in it, but mostly yards of blank pages. It's a start. No one is particularly interested in my escapades. People have been busy with their own projects. A cohort in my Army Reserve unit have completed sports parachuting courses—they can't stop talking about it—and one is still in Kenya on safari. Another is filming a TV commercial where tens of skydivers link up in mid-air to promote a lifestyle product. We call him the "Stuntman".

Still another has returned from Cyprus and tells us about the opportunities there, working, but also sunning on beaches we haven't heard of. The roll call completes with someone starting work at a gym on the King's Road. It's a smorgasbord of riches.

In the drill hall at the barracks, I look at the training programme and see there is a weekend away coming up and write the date in my diary. Feeling pangs of guilt, back home, I check my syllabus, and look for my notes. In my War and Defence Studies class, I'm studying the Battle for Goose Green in the Falklands, and certain failures in command and control.

But my attention wanders to the promise of a weekend trip out of London meeting up with Rachael, after I've sorted out my studies.

## 15 CATCHING UP

I t's a bright day in the West End of London, but what's left of winter still refuses to loosen its grip on the capital. I grab the Tube from Tottenham Court Road to Oxford Circus, taking the exit stairs up, two steps at a time, emerging into the spring sunshine, striding past the newspaper seller at the top handing out the morning edition of the *Evening Standard*. On the way into campus, I remind myself I need to take stock of my course notes in the library, near one of the grand, imposing stone buildings in Portland Place, right next to the BBC.

I am ashamed to admit that having missed classes, I've got to place myself at the mercy of my fellow course members and ask to borrow notes. I walk into the library and spy one of the girls, Mary. She wears a pair of light blue, cuffed Levi's jeans, and a mustard-coloured jumper, with brown hair parted in the middle. She is sitting at a middle table, not at a cloistered booth on the side.

"Hi there, Mary," I call.

She looks up.

"Alright. How was the sailing you were doing?" she replies.

"It was good. I can get a job crewing pretty much anywhere," I reply.

"And how's that friend you were talking about?" she asks next.

"Okay, we're meeting up, we've both been busy."

"What was her name again?"

"Rachael."

"That was it, she's pretty. Cool," she says. "Hey, how are you going with the European Law essay?" she asks, flicking her hair back and readjusting the tie.

"No problem, I'm almost done. Need any help?"

"I'm struggling actually, I don't get it…it's so annoying–you're good at Law," she says, grumbling.

Maybe I am not, but I realise this is a chance to trade: I understand *Defrenne v Sabena*, the well-known Industrial Relations case, and a myriad of other precedents from other cases, handed down by the European Law Court at Strasbourg. I've worked out how to apply them to example cases in class, earning the nod from our lecturer.

"Yup, I wing it, you know I do," I reply.

I look down at the table and see immaculate notes, colour-coded, on ruled margin, with legible, cursive, bubble-writing for the win.

"Er, Mary, I don't suppose there's any chance I could borrow your notes? I missed that week, as you know. I'll help you with the assignment."

"Sure, take them."

"Okay, I'll copy them now, then I'll help with the essay."

*Bingo.*

It's easy to stand at the photocopier and run off copies and replace the notes back on the table. I sit down next to Mary and reach into my bag to get my text, and find a blue biro in my jacket pocket, lid missing, but there's no ink down my white Lee t-shirt.

"Right. *Sabena v the European Court of Justice*," I say. *Time to uphold my side of the bargain.*

I take her over the salient points, showing her the relevant paragraphs in the text and the court case. She puts on a pair of Discman headphones, and I leave her to focus on touching up her essay.

I reflect on what a poor student I am. Simply devouring the textbooks from the course list wasn't going to get me across the line. It was not that I couldn't pass exams—on the contrary, I could, cramming the week before and winging it—it's just that I struggled with attending day-to-day lectures and seminars. It wasn't me—I felt like a fraud. *It didn't occupy me. I didn't care enough.*

I liked my lecturer in my War and Defence Studies classes, who wore horn-rimmed glasses and natty tweed jackets over lavender shirts. He held my interest as he talked about the rise of China, their interest in the Spratly islands in the South China Sea and explained the concept of Mutually Assured Destruction in nuclear warfare.

"Want to go for a coffee, Steve?" Mary is looking up, smiling.

"Let's go next door."

We step outside into the London street, Mary adjusting her scarf, and we find a coffee shop and enter with a peal from the doorbell. We sip tepid lattes and talk about plans before it's time to part ways.

"See you Steve, enjoy the weekend."

# 16 ON THE FLATS

I 've spent a fair bit of time out in the wet and wild National parks away from the safe haven of the M25 London Orbital. France, Italy, New Zealand and even Australia have their Alpine regions with sheer peaks and meadows with wildflowers. England and Wales take the somewhat more modest route, no peak higher than 1,080 metres, if you leave out ambitious Scotland. I scaled Pen-y-Fan a couple of Easters ago in the Welsh hills and I found it a hot and sweaty labour. But you don't have to go high to feel adventurous. Some of the most challenging terrain in England can be found on the moors.

I'm on Exmoor now, the cold and blustering land that sits where the West Country joins the rest of the UK. It's flat, but in winter, the wind blows across it with a keenness to tap the unwary.

We're in a pub near Tiverton, recovering from the cold that has seeped through the waxed outer of a Barbour and through several woolen jumpers. Even lunch has not let us dry out completely. Rachael has a cheeky grin. She is not that far from home, and has made it over in her old Citroën to join us for a ride out.

"Don't you just love it out here, Steve?" she asks me, smoothing out her jodhpurs.

In the pub, there's a terrific open fire in the corner with old, russet-coloured bricks and a worn, smoothed out mantelpiece with copper irons suspended over it. Our ride leader is sitting on a stool, head down, working out how long she can sit in front of the coals before she calls time on us. An elderly local dressed in musty tweed from head to toe sits opposite, pipe in hand, I am guessing contemplating the fact he is in no better place in the time *he* has left. He rustles a page of the *Daily Telegraph* and coughs loudly.

A member of the bar staff pads over and lobs a piece of wood on to the coals from a little stack in the corner, and sparks and ashes fly up in front of our faces. We stare at it, transfixed.

I'm nursing a pint of Caffreys, my thighs sore, from where my saddle has rubbed. I'm watching our leader, so I know when it's time. Every time she looks at her watch, I check mine.

We're part of a riding group based out of a farm which organises holidays. A piano tuner of my acquaintance, Nigel, drove me down there on Friday evening in his green Vauxhall Cavalier. If he's not tuning the Princess of Wales's piano at St James's palace, he's wanting to get out of London like I am. We took the motorway out of the Capital, and down dark country lanes before the night drew in, badgers and wildlife scampering off back to their burrows and digs. The accommodation is basic, but they've turned on the heating as they know we are coming down.

My interest in riding arose from a friend who talked about it. Other friends reckoned it was a bit girly, but I couldn't agree, and I spent enough time with gear and equipment as it was. Anyone can ride a bike, but to learn to work with an animal was something else. I started in a school in North London with the university club and volunteered to help muck out the stables in my own time over the vacation before getting any sort of competency.

The ride leader looks at her watch again. Time to pay a visit to the men's room. It's one of those cold and draughty outhouses with properly filthy and indecent cartoons on the walls depicting country people doing what country people do, flirting and fornicating. There are men and women in states of undress, caught *in flagrante*, men with engorged members; women with large chests. The men wear deerstalker hats, jerkins and wellington boots, in full country regalia from a bygone age. On the other wall are rather more classic prints of country scenes.

Walking back past the main bar, it's obvious the pub doesn't think much of the European Union's plan to introduce a single currency, and Germany and France are targets of locals' venom. I stop at cuttings of newspapers and pinned-up letters to local Members of Parliament, listing the risks to the country life, thumbing their noses up at the Westminster bureaucracy. Does the fact I live in London mean I am part of the problem?

The ride leader stands. Time to mount up. We put on damp, steaming, waxed jackets. I don't have a Barbour jacket, only an old M65 field jacket. The older gents in our party have the means to kit themselves out in glorious gear, including expensive leather boots. Mine are rubber, on sale from Millets.

In the carpark, we untie our horses' lead ropes, and walk them to a gap in the hedge: they pace energetically and their hooves clatter on the tarmac. We help each other mount, stiffly, and ask our steeds to walk past the four-wheel drives and sedans, out through a gate on to a right of way across a farmer's field.

The moor stretches out in front of us—barren, in the main, with clustered trees and bush scattered about providing scant cover. It's undulating and bleak.

We walk towards a copse, swaying in that four-time, standing in the stirrups for our mounts to relieve themselves. The forlorn trees stand proud, and I can spot flattish terrain, good for a canter. Our horses circle, on controlled reins, waiting for the opportunity to let loose. As the wind picks up, our ride leader turns around, and waits for the rear of the ride to catch up.

"Everyone ready?" she says.

She doesn't wait for a response and with a kick, takes off.

I give my horse free rein and barely need to ask for trot or canter. We race off in pursuit, and I lean forward, heels pressing down, elbows in, with my chin held over her head. The rain comes in sideways, stinging my cheeks and eyes.

The field is petering out at a hedgerow, but we know what to expect. One by one, we jump cleanly, airborne for an instant, landing sure-footedly. (It's only after, I realise that's the first in a while, *and,* I've stayed on, too.)

We halt to rest. There's a jangle of bits and there are foam speckles at our horses' mouths. We can canter along a gentle, graded, downhill path lined with trees and a mat of composting mucky leaves—accompanied by the mellifluous sound of pounding hooves. It's warmer out of the wind, and I jerk down on the ring-pull zip on my jacket, taking a hand off the reins.

When we get back, we amble stiffly from the stable area back to our rooms, peeling off sodden jackets, and jodhpurs and change in to dry clobber. Supper out will be welcome, but first we stretch tired muscles in the living room. *Baywatch* is on the TV with the sound off. Nicole Eggert walks along the beach, swinging her Hollywood hips and pouting. Rachel looks at me and laughs. David Hasselhoff is doing his usual act, which is being David Hasselhoff. To me, he's still the 1980s hero of *Knightrider*.

We find ourselves in a rustic pub in a local town on the edge of the moor. The waitress wears a black skirt and white blouse, fit for all seasons. She takes our orders, stood to, attentively, at the head of the table. I choose the beef Wellington, lean back in my chair, and study the clientele without making it too obvious. If I judge correctly, it's mostly retired solicitors and farmers.

"That bloke looks like he's sold a London business and bought up half the 'Buy to Lets' in the village," Nigel whispers, "he looks like he's seen better days."

Bit of a people-watcher is Nigel.

I share a glass of red wine in the sitting room with Rachael, and she sits in her thermals, feet out to the fire with her wool socks drying out on the fire irons. I can't help but note how pretty her feet are and hope she doesn't notice me look. We talk about life and work, our dreams for the future.

*We are getting along just fine.*

"Come back and visit me in a few weekends," she announces.

"I'd love to, Rachael!" I gush.

"Call me."

And she gives me a peck on the cheek.

But first, there's the small hurdle of semester examinations scheduled over the course of the week. A small crowd of undergrads jostle at the board when the slots are pinned up by the faculty administrator. She's a pretty, mousy-haired girl who studied here, but never quite managed to leave the faculty. There are groans when people realise they have two exams in one day, and also sighs of delight,

"I've got two days in between, though, to cram," someone says.

On the day of the European Law exam, there's a line of students at the exam room door waiting to be let in by the invigilator. I join the back of the queue as others arrive and push past the line to where their friends are standing. Mary chats to hide her nerves. I scan my crib notes. I write these down on the top of my paper as soon as I find a table.

"You may start now," announces the invigilator, looking almost smug.

She settles down to read a paperback she has brought to while away the hours.

I grab a pen and pick off the questions I will tackle, and with no time to lose, I crack on with writing—I'm in turbo mode. There is silence in the room with nothing but the ticking of a clock, sounds of pen on paper, muted coughs and gasps, or the sound of a water bottle top cracked off. Outside, the occasional horn from the street as London W1 continues despite us.

"Please finish your last sentence," intones the invigilator when time is up.

I remember my sentence can be as long as it needs to be, and by the use of judicious semi-colons, and a colon, I am able to muster and arrange my conclusion artfully. Outside, classmates group to compare and contrast the questions they have tackled, and share their agony. I am content to wait and see what happens.

I reward myself by scouring the Top 20 chart albums display at the HMV flagship store in Piccadilly and choosing *I should Coco* by Supergrass. On the tube, I unfurl the wrapping from a Big Mac, take a bite, and look up at the adverts on the Bakerloo line train. So, on reflection: maybe I *could* cope with the business of studying, but it wasn't really what I wanted to be doing. There's

Rachael, for one thing. I'd love to see her again.

## 17 GET BACK ON THE HORSE

There's a trill in the hallway. I get up from the sofa in front of the TV with a grunt and pad on the icy lino over there. The phone is on top of a pile of address books with numbers scrawled on the covers, and I stretch for it before the caller rings off.

"It's Rachael. Alright?" she says in her mezzo-soprano. It's like she's in the room.

I smile enthusiastically, my heart racing, and cradle the receiver in my neck, forgetting the cold for now.

"Right," I reply. "How have you been?"
We chat for a bit. Then the invite drops:

"Come down to the country! I'm not busy this weekend. Got nothing on."

I drive down the M4 towards Bath and the West in my ageing Ford Escort at 85 miles per hour the whole way. Part of the old dashboard is loose, and there is an annoying resonance as I hug the centre lane. It's not important.

Rachael's grandfather owns a farm on the edge of the Cotswolds, and Rachael is occupying a tiny worker's cottage. She greets me in the driveway wearing a pair of jeans, boots, and a pilled-up jumper, hair in a loose bob. She gives me a tour. A small garden leads into a kitchen which has been whipped into a vision of rusticity, with a solid wooden bench; a tiny sitting room with William Morris antiques (a narrow staircase spirals up to a bedroom), and a bathroom you can barely turn around in. Upstairs, there's an immaculate nook with a window seat to read in, and there are some broken-spined paperbacks.

She pulls me to the window and points out the villages scattered over the valleys and hills.

"Let's explore town," she says.
Grabbing a warm coat, she leads me down the path to the

road.

We giggle and chat, and I ask after our friends in the US and England. We look at souvenir shops and browse in clothes boutiques. She draws closer at times and pats my bottom playfully when I say something silly. We laugh at my stupid London questions, and shop assistants smile accommodatingly.

She tells me about Bermuda. Her father is a banker there, and she has spent most of her years there enjoying the way of life. I can't imagine what it must be like to live there in foreign latitudes and climes. It makes my goal to get to the Caribbean Sea all the more alluring.

Back at the house, she says,

"You hungry Steve? I'll make you a sandwich."

She obligingly pops bacon in the microwave for a brunch and passes me the BBQ sauce.

In the evening, we head over to the pub for a drink and bag chairs by a crackling fire in a stone hearth. We both enjoy our pints and get closer and closer. She gets us another, we have several. Her little touches become frequent. We leave before chucking out time and walk back along the street to the house. There is no one about at this late hour. We stagger to a bench and stop for a bit. I lean in at the door. She giggles and comes close for a tantalising kiss, looks in my eyes, then turns with her key and gets the door open.

We sway upstairs to the nook off the landing. She leans over for a bottle of Vodka from a cabinet, and I take the bottle and pour a drink for us. She takes a sip from hers, and I set mine down, place hers with it, and take her in my arms, kissing her. She sidles up close. Our tongues find each other, and I place my hands on her hips, then the small of her back. Her eyes close, and her breathing quickens. I reach under her jumper, and I hear a muffled ping as I unhook her bra strap. She murmurs. I decide to not take things too far this time and save a bit for another time.

"Good night..." I say, and we slowly pull apart.

The next morning, I sneak up to her room and slip into bed with her, snuggling under the bedclothes. She is sleepy and warm under an elaborate system of quilts and blankets, and we doze for a while.

We rise and go downstairs. After toast, and a cup of steaming Earl Grey, we walk over to local stables, and she offers me a horse belonging to a friend, and we ride down the hill through country lanes in the sunshine. She greets local people who are out in their front gardens trimming hedges or pottering about. It's a world away from London and only two hours away at the same time.

They say that you are not a bona fide rider until you've fallen off. I've put this notion to a few of the riders I know, and they say it's true.

I have never come off a horse, so I can't properly make any claims. But when we canter across parkland, I lose my seat and shift alarmingly sideways, and after a few strides I can't recover, and I know I am going to go. I understand it's best to not fight this, and I succumb to the inevitable. I hit the soft earth, which takes my fall and I land on my side. No damage done—I've only got to brush the dried mud off my jodhpurs. Rachael reins in at my side, peering down with a smirk on her face.

"Get back on the horse!" Rachael implores.

I'm just relieved it didn't hurt.

"You ok, Steve?" she chuckles at my predicament.

We head back out to a different pub. It's a cold night, and we sit close. After sipping pints, we negotiate the winding lanes back to the house.

*Those eyes.*

With no words spoken, we head into the bedroom, and take off our clothes simultaneously, saying nothing, leaving them on the floor. I think she is gorgeous.

We sleep in, and rise to hangovers—but taking note of the "hair of the dog"—we find ourselves back in the pub by evening's end. I decide not to get back on the road to London for classes. I'll miss the first day of the week.

*Maybe I'm falling for her, I don't know. Does she feel the same way about me?*

I'm sorry to have to leave her, and she says goodbye. I get a passerby to capture a photo of us loved up, arms around each other.

"You seem to have a busy life, are you going to have time for me?" she says.

"Of course," I say. "Besides, I think you're great. I'll *make* time."

"So are you!" She gives me a hug.

"Write *soon*," she says.

"I will."

*Now there's a promise.*

I return, back to the London bustle and decide that all is well with the world. I can finish my degree course and keep training, living and loving. I just need to manage it as best I can.

# 18 UPS AND DOWNS

I t's still cold, even though it's April. The early buds and blossom are struggling, and people are back peering in the travel agency windows at cheap end of season flights to warmer places—destinations in Spain and in the Canaries. I can't say I blame them.

I'm away with my platoon, practicing our shooting. We are housed in old barracks near Edinburgh. It's bizarre to be back in Scotland and I relinquish the opportunity to get out of London again. We are staying within cooee of the town with its rising hill to the castle.

Some of us have developed a bit of a cough, as the rooms are unheated. It's like my childhood, when the ice formed on the inside of the windowpane overnight. It's hard getting out of bed, as our bare feet are cold on the ground heading to the showers, which thankfully are piping hot. Shaving is over in double-quick time. The bloke next to me shaves the back of his neck in neat, practised, upward swipes against the grain, and breaks wind extravagantly. It's good to get over to breakfast where there's central heating.

Our training captain cuts a dash: he wears a vee-collared wool sweater and corduroy trousers, which he pairs with a shirt and coarse knitted dress tie, collar stays visible inside the pressed cotton. His hair is parted immaculately, like a Second World War battle hero. He lays on a trip to Alnwick castle over the border. We wander around the grounds, looking at the battlements. We pretend to read the plinths and signs and we laugh when men slip on the icy steps. But all told, we'd prefer to be chatting in the minibus.

*I need a coffee.*

It's a fun day out. There's a chance to have a gab to each other, tell jokes, swan around and do something different.

Our sergeant opens the classroom door, and a captain puts his head around the frame.

"Listen up." He gets our attention, and the room falls silent. The training major is behind him, smiling.

"We're not driving back to London, there's a lob on. We're parachuting back into England. No move before 1400 hours."

The sergeant closes the door.

The room erupts. The diehard parachuting tragics whoop, grandstand and look excited. The rest of us reflect on the task in hand and wind ourselves up for the effort. It's not just the best exit we can muster from the C-130 Hercules cargo plane, it's the preparation we need to do.

We will spend hours at the Royal Air Force base carefully packing our gear until it's "fit to fly". The loadmasters don't want our gear coming adrift whilst we are approaching the exit door. It's a guarantee our pilots will fly back over the Lake District, or North Wales, to practise low-level flying below radar before coming up to drop height at 800 feet (240 metres) which is not much. It will be a bumpy ride. The mortar boys will have to parachute with their mortar tubes and bases, and others are scratching their heads, considering their loads.

"Who's on which plane?" says my section commander.

"Tactical loading," he reminds us.

I feel nervous. This means we will spread out in different planes. The Army wants to ensure a single company is not wiped out in an instant.

"We'll still have to bus it from the west, back to London," someone points out. In other words, we won't save much time.

I reflect on the risks. There's the chance of a mid-air collision with another parachutist outside the aircraft, an entanglement with another parachute, or a hard landing. If I fail to jump cleanly, I'll get twists in my rigging lines and will lose control of my parachute. We won't get much sleep, but there will be opportunity on the tarmac next to the aircraft before we emplane.

Two hours later, the sergeant sticks his head around the door. "It's off guys, wind's too high for the jump!"

*Bugger.*

The room is deflated.

*God, my tooth hurts.*

One of my molars has been giving me trouble all day, a dull throb which puts me off my work. It's not the pain of a knife cut, or a blow—only that constant gnaw which gets inside you, always present, never abating.

After breakfast, rather than head to the platoon office, I head off to the base dentist to see what he can do. I'm seen promptly—business is quiet. He gets a light and peers into the corner of my mouth I point to, craning forward. I am aware he has a touch of halitosis—ironic, I conclude. I await the verdict.

"You have an abscess!" he announces, almost accusative in tone. I don't get a chance to answer.

"That's coming out now," he adds, equally aggressively.

The nurse does not disagree and will be complicit in his next act.

He gets to work, and she attends, handing him the tools of the trade—carpentry comes to mind. There is a grinding noise—I'm in no pain, but I can feel the cracking of roots in my jawline. The tooth is handed to me, like an indignant souvenir—and my mouth fills with the taste of salty brine. The nurse gives me a pad for the wound and half a toilet roll.

I arrive back at my platoon a bit miffed and show the crew a mouthful of blood, like a blood-sucking zombie. It's hard focusing on training. The pain in my mouth is just as bad, if not worse. In the bathroom, I stare into the mirror, trying to work out how to deal with the recurrent throb in my jaw. At lunch, I call Rachael and she tuts. It's hard to gauge the sympathy.

"A civilian dentist would have saved that tooth," she says." They can't be bothered, those guys. Bad luck."

This does nothing to cheer me up.

*Great.*

"But anyway, see you next weekend," she adds.

We move back down south. We are out shooting on the urban warfare ranges looking down from an Observation Post at a mocked-up streetscape representing a town. The idea is to identify the terrorists and not shoot civilians. Doors open and close, men appear at windows, or is it a young man with his baby sister in his arms? We go through this drill in small teams, several times over, until we're comfortable. I discover I'm a quick "battle" shot, but I hit a "good guy" and have a hard think about what could happen if the exercise was for real.

"I need you to look back at that," says the platoon commander, punching me in the chest to make his point.

Our time concludes with an assault on a training village on Salisbury Plain which the battalion attacks after a long approach march in the early hours before dawn. By the time we have found our way into the streets, we are finding the lack of sleep catching up with us. Small consolation—at least this time there are no TV cameras around.

Last summer, I found myself at a street corner, shooting, rapid-fire into a house, in front of a TV crew which I hadn't noticed until then. It was a bit distracting at the time, but amusing to watch on tv, one night later in the year. There seemed to be no escape from the scrutiny. At a break, I had been standing around gazing wearily into the distance, and glanced down to find a journalist training a camera with a long lens on me getting shots. She even came over with a release form. I thought it nice of her to ask.

# 19 A CALL FROM GERMANY

*To young men contemplating a voyage, I would say go.* Joshua Slocum

I've returned from Rachael's house late. We enjoyed the weekend together, and cemented our relationship. We ate out one night in a restaurant—lasagna for me, risotto for her, then sat in the next. We cooked a meal, and I grabbed a candle and sat it on the table between us. I admired the way the light flickered across her face whilst we chatted and made plans. We resumed where we left off; walked around Cheltenham—looked at the shops we hadn't seen together, ate, drunk, laughed and slept before I finally joined the conga line of traffic on the M4—getting back late to London due to weekend roadworks. Lectures had my name on them that week.

Midweek, I am watching our newly installed cable TV clicking up and down the range of stations on offer, when I get a call from a random stranger, only perhaps not so random. It's Knut from Dusseldorf, Germany, inviting me to come and crew on his yacht *Derelict,* across the Atlantic at the end of the year. He's seen my name on a crewing list.

I visualise a six-foot blond present and correct German man, putting aside for now any international Anglo-Teutonic rivalry. We will be joined by other Germans, another Brit, a Swede, and others will arrive later. I flick a pizza menu off the top of the phone books and jot down his details. We chat briefly: facts, destinations and financials. He asks me for an email address and fax, and I oblige.

When I awake, I discover a plethora of warm sheets of A4 have coiled up on the floor next to our printer and I find myself looking at the boat, itinerary, plans and crew with mounting excitement. Knut has included a plan view of *Derelict,* and very impressive she looks too, on paper. Surely, this is an opportunity too good to pass up for any other others that may come my way. A bird in the hand is worth two in the bush, as they say. I decide I will join, and fax back my decision to meet the group in Las Palmas, lying my passport down flat under the glass to provide my details. I haven't quite got the funds for the travel though, but I have plenty of time to find the cash.

When I tell Rachael, she remembers I was planning something on these lines when we met on Exmoor.

"So, you will be leaving me then? We won't be seeing much of each other. I mean, you *are* off a lot at the weekends," she counters.

"Well, yes, but it's not even eight weeks," I explain.

"Hang on, though, you said you were a bit short of cash."

"I'll sort something, Rachael," I reply. "I get a bonus from the military if I do enough training."

There's that incentive begging.

***

There's a bakery in the high street which has been doing a roaring trade to locals for generations; a sign tells us so—and I decide today's the day my student funds will stretch to a fresh croissant. I find the bakery in the small parade of shops. I can smell a delightful aroma of sugar and oven-baking and I stand briefly to take it in, in the fug of the ovens and heat lamps over the counters. The shop assistant bags my pastry, and I pay for it from a collection of loose change.

I grab a cup of tea and stand outside, quickly looking up and down. The street narrows into a single pavement where people can barely pass. My local National Westminster bank is sited here in a Grade One listed building. It's nine am, and the bank is due to open in a tick. I steep the tea bag in my takeaway cup, and it oozes tannin like an octopus in fright-mode.

I notice the branch manager as soon as he opens the door and flips the sign from "Closed" to "Open". He recognises me as we've chatted over the years.

"Hi Steve–er Mr Malins, great to see you. You've got an appointment. Come through now."

I follow him into his glass-walled office, a drab utilitarian affair with a table, and power leads snaking along the skirting board of the wall. I sit down opposite to him, and he logs in to his computer.

*Let business commence.*

"So you want a short-term loan? Well, for a student, you've actually got a good credit rating. That's one of the best student accounts I've seen for a while. You've managed it well, it seems. There's no problem in me extending you a small loan," he says.

*Bingo.* That will be all the Army Reserve money I earn.

"Great, appreciated," I respond.

"In fact, your credit score is an eight, that's not bad at all," he says, raising his eyebrows.

"Good to hear, I had no idea."

"Okay, sign here, and I'll get the funds dispersed once we're done here."

I walk out of the branch having solved the cash flow issue— with the money to fund my flights to get me to the Canaries and back to the UK, and expenses for food—and, based on my cash flow and obligations, I'll have the loan cleared within months of getting back in the New Year.

I stroll back past the bakery, and stop at the travel agent, a small bespoke outfit half-way home near a playhouse. I push the door and walk in. I've checked the flights in the back of the *Sunday Times,* but I reckon local businesses can do better this far out from departure. I wait my turn in a foam-backed plastic chair down the back.

The girl on duty stands and asks me to come forward to sit at her desk, and she sits back down, smoothing her dress over her knees. After tapping away on her keyboard looking at a green screen, taking sips of tea, she gets me a charter to Las Palmas and back from Saint Lucia to London. So that's the flights sorted. I call Rachael the next day, and she interrupts the work she is doing on a tender to chat.

"It's organised then!" she says, sounding upbeat. "Good."

I outline the plan: like an elevator pitch. The crew will meet the 3$^{rd}$ weekend in November, in Las Palmas, slipping our moorings the last weekend for the epic Atlantic crossing. That gives us a week to victual and prepare.

# 20 THE TIDEWAY

The news that the exam results are in at the faculty spreads like wildfire. I visit the brown-haired faculty administrator sitting at the counter with my heart in my mouth. Glancing up from the VDU, and her usual work, she passes me a laser printout. I take a peek, and note I have passed them all, except for one. I've graded Lower Second for most, where I reckon I deserve to be, but I score a Higher Second for Criminal Law. Overall, I am par for the course. As for the failure—she reminds me I am allowed to flunk one exam per year, as long as I've got a high enough grade to have "taken" it. I decide to bank this setback and move on.

"Well done, Steve," Rachael says, when I call her from the cool hallway that night. "You made it happen."

Things were moving—and it seemed my newfound water skills were back in demand, and maybe even consolidating. I was not the landlubber I thought I had always been: I'm coxing the girl's rowing team and rowing myself.

One day at college, later in the evening, I had walked to the top floor of the library where an impromptu meeting was being held by the Rowing club.

"Hey!" said a girl wearing a yellow fleece, with a black bob, as I ambled over to their table to see what they were up to.

"You look fit. Do you want to row, and cox our boat?"

Always keen for a new challenge, I had agreed.

I enjoy my time in the club even though I knew nothing about rowing: we have ridiculously competent rowers from clubs all over England (and at least one American with a crew cut, *avant garde* for early 1995). Our club house is in Chiswick on the Thames, and two garage-sized storage areas house our boats. A small bar on the first floor overlooks the water. The club is based on the Middlesex county side of the river looking over the Surrey side. There was lots of lingo to learn.

"Steve, this part of the Thames is called the 'Tideway'. It's where the river is tidal—as it flows from the estuary mouth down to Teddington lock," says coach.

I nod.

Our coach is a graduate of medium height with a huge amount of hair, in fact, you could say it is almost an afro. We meet once a week for training. On one occasion, he sends groups of us out to lap the track where I can shine, beating the whole club to the finish line.

Like sailing, there are special terms for everything. We have "eights" where men and women crews row eight up, with a cox steering from the back. The front man is known as "bow", but "stroke" is at the back—they are a stroke (touch) away from the cox. The cox steers and calls out the effort needed, in "reps" needed as a race continues. And, we have "fours", and even single sculls for the introverts who want to row "one-up".

One late afternoon, we head out from the boathouse and row up towards central London, passing various landmarks: the Stag Brewery, Fullers Brewery, St Paul's school; and the Harrods depository. (What happens there, I wonder?) I'm satisfied the combination of seeing the old brick edifices and chimneys of the breweries and no small amount of physical hard work for the crew is going to earn us a drink in the clubhouse later.

It was always amusing to watch nearby clubs pass by on the water. Training went on for a while, and there were no toilet breaks—you had to go before you went, like your teacher told you at school. Dying to go, mischievous boys would stand up in their boats and relieve themselves over the side, timing this opportunity funnily enough, when they were in full view of a clubhouse and an ensemble of unsuspecting onlookers. High jinks all round, even if the girls weren't particularly impressed. On warmer days, as summer approached, I found the lapping of the water against the sides of the boat rather sleep-inducing, and there were more than a couple of occasions when I woke up to hear:

"Steve, Hammersmith Bridge!": at the last minute, I steered us safely from the majestic stone piers.

I also had to get to grips with such arcane theory of the tide, the water rushing in or out of the river, from or to the estuary. To race quickly, you had to be in the middle with it, using it to your advantage, or along the shores, avoiding it. The tide rose up and down twice a day. It was worth knowing what time of day the tide changed, the "turn", before you set out. There was always an informed bright spark who knew.

This also leads to a wider social life. At the world-famous Henley Regatta, it was a lot less about the rowing and far more about the refreshment—liquid refreshment—in the shape of wine and champers. We set up in a tent and made our way through drinks and nibbles all afternoon. By the early evening, people were hanging over the tent guy ropes. Then there were the invites to club members' houses.

One night was at a little terrace in Camden, off the high street, full of cigarette and pot haze, bottles of spirits on the kitchen counter and cans of lager. Someone had put CDs on with the multi-stack player in the cramped front-room. We got through cheap blended whiskies and progressed to shots. Inebriated, I sit in the kitchen with one of my teammate's London friends, and we chat. She asks me if I have a girlfriend.

"Yes, I do," I tell her.

I am in the ground floor faculty library, head down, concentrating—well I can kid myself, can't I? In fact, I've just put down my International Political Economy class approved textbook with an irritated grimace. The rowing coach, rather more anonymous away from the club, walks over in a pair of Nike trainers and cords.

"Steve."

"Hi mate. What's happening?" I reply.

"There's a race on in a few weeks. Can you make it?"

"Sure I can, no dramas."

The Head of the River race takes place around April each year, and every Tom, Dick and Harry descends on the section of the Thames called the Head. Most people will have heard of the famous annual Oxford versus Cambridge boat race, where the "dark blues" and "light blues" race on a course a smidge over four miles, from Putney to Mortlake. My father was evacuated to Cambridge in the Second World War—so he goes for Cambridge, the rest of the family go for Oxford with our family connection.

This race goes in the opposite direction, starting at Mortlake and it's everyone else rowing, so clubs like ours. In the Bell and Crown at Chiswick, I find myself next to the Great Britain cox who won Olympic Gold with Steve Redgrave and Matthew Pinsett in 1992 and then went on to do it again in 1996 and 2000. He indulges me, and we get a photo together, grinning like loons.

Rachael thinks all these stories are a hoot.

\*\*\*

I've got essays to write and get through, which involve trips up in the lift to the top-floor of the library and a favoured spot between the stacks and an area that catches the light. I have a batch of texts in my bag, and I grab one trying to find the obscure reference I reckon will help me make a major point in my narrative. My grandfather once sat an exam in the late 1920s, and decided there was not one question he thought he could tackle. He picked the most likely one and began:

*"Far be it from me to answer a question on the mechanics of this matter, but surely I can bring your attention to this other matter I have here, that is more important".*

*So much for answering the question, Grandpa.*

Despite that debacle, he still matriculated. It dawns on me that no wonder he missed out on the Bishop of Oxford slot. It's also not clear to me right now, whether I will manage the same feat—to pass at the end of this year.

A siren sounds outside, outside in the street, and the London Fire Brigade shoots past, blues and twos going. This is just the distraction I need from my work and getting up, I stand with my thumbs in my belt hoops and watch the second truck weave past a car and towards Oxford Circus.

My focus flits to an upcoming "jolly" away from lectures and essays. I check my organiser, and leafing to the calendar, check an entry highlighted, and circled:

*Switzerland Training Camp*

Everyone in the rowing club was buzzing about this trip to the Alps. It is an opportunity to get out of the UK further afield for us all. We were leaving next week.

# 21 LIKE CLOCKWORK

It was light when we got on the ferry at Dover, and still the small hours of the morning, when we disembarked in Oostende on the other side of the English Channel. We had congregated near one a bar and contemplated the price of beer and food on our student incomes and slept, coiled up on chairs or couches. The floor worked just as well. Coach delegated drivers for the two minibuses we have borrowed from the student union.

We join the highway heading down through Belgium and France, and anyone awake cranes to look at motorway signs to see which country we are in for the present. As it gets lighter, the chatter increases as people wake from slumber to peer around. Some of the girls complain about the lack of material comforts in the back of the minibus and fidget in their seats, lamenting the hardship.

"These seats are so hard," one says.

"Need a shower," another grumbles.

The sky lightens in the east and those of us who were not dozing were delighted to see—and share—the fact there's a sign naming the German-name city of Wankdorf, just inside the Swiss border. The sun does not provide any warmth until we hit the main highway in Switzerland when it comes slanting in through the passenger's side.

Most of us have heard of Lake Lucerne, but there's a smaller lake, an hour closer, called the SarnerSee. That's our destination and it comes into view. It's impressive to look at—a large lake over three miles long. As we speed down the road alongside, we look across to the other side. The grey frigid waters look cold.

"We're going to be accommodated overlooking the water," remarks Coach as we take the winding corners and climb the crests.

"It's got to be a mile across," our driver says, glancing over.

He swings the wheel over with the heel of his hand and turns into an alley between buildings, and parks up. Our accommodation is a brick two-storey villa across the road from the lake.

"Hang on guys, let's see what's happening before we get out."

Our driver talks to the driver in the lead vehicle and then returns.

"Okay, see those storage sheds—the shells are going in those now. We'll take them down to the water tomorrow. First thing."

Despite our weariness, we manhandle the boats off the trailers and manouevre them into the sheds, and we form a human chain to carry packs and gear inside the villa through a back door with an awkward step. As there's a nip in the air, we fish bobble hats and gloves out of the transport.

From windows on the first-floor landing, we size up our new training location.

Pastureland falls away down to the lake shore scattered with cottages and outbuildings. There's the occasional resident cow, or pig, and a stable. The water is extensive and stretches left, and right towards Lucerne. Across the water, there are ever-green conifers and mountains with cornices of melting snow. There's a particularly high peak which dominates the others.

"There are ski resorts up there," Richard says, squinting.

The crew seem to think our new location is right out of the book and 1980s TV series *Heidi,* and they make sure they get plenty of mileage out of this witticism. It's going to be the wisecrack of the week.

There's a babble of excitement, and everyone bags a bottom or top bunk in a dorm, girls on one side of the well-worn carpeted landing, boys on the other. I share with Richard, one of our amenable, muscular rowers plus an American guest with the short haircut—Keanu Reeves has made cropped hair fashionable again in this year's hit-movie *Speed.* Most of the boys favour 1990s quiffs and bigger hair.

\*\*\*

The keen people amongst us are up early for breakfast—but in our room, most of the blokes sleep in and scramble late, going down dishevelled. We send a driver to the nearest train station to pick up a girl who has been in France for the holidays and has joined by rail. They arrive back with her gear and the driver takes me aside:

"Funny. You see these teenagers walking on the concourse with guns strapped to their packs at the station," he recounts.

"Those young men will be Swiss militia or soldiers," I reply knowledgably. "The Swiss have always maintained their neutrality, but most families have military training–they keep rifles at home."

It's different from the sober system we have in the UK.

We retrieve our boats from the store and walk them down to the jetty on the lake, giggling, and manhandle them on to the water, wellington boots abandoned and strewn on the grass.

Later, we see our boys in their boat, and girls in theirs, out in the lake encircled with tentacles of mist. Higher up the shore, this mist persisted, and higher still were the snow-capped crags of the mountains. A perfect Swiss scene. At this altitude, out on the water, it was cool, but the sun shone, and many of the crews catch rays on their outings when they strip down to singlets, beanies on their heads, to rest their stretched arms and cool their shoulders.

Coach wants to check what the girls are up to.

"Steve–let's go and see how the girls are getting on."

We head on to the lake in a spare launch with an outboard. He has one hand on the tiller, the other handles a megaphone. The team are looking good, looking cohesive. They take strokes in time from Coach's cadence, staring in to the middle-distance, their biceps straining and chins jutting out, focusing on the slide, their seats hitting the backstops at the same time. I've got a camera and get a few shots of them and the snow-capped peaks.

At tea break, we mill around on the jetty looking at the vista. Most of the club are sitting in twos and threes. I lounge with my roommates, left ankle on right knee, shielding my eyes from the glare. Richard glances over.

"Steve. That ski resort over the valley," he says.

Richard has skied before and can't wait to go again.

"Never been mate," I say.

"Doesn't matter, you'll work it out."

He gives me an impromptu ski lesson in the kitchen of the accommodation, our cups of tea safely on the table.

"Lean forward, shins against your boots. That's basically it. To turn, just unweight a ski. And slow down using the snowplough."

He demonstrates a "pizza slice" shape with his toes angled in, which I copy.

"That's it," he concludes.

We get a lift to the resort, which is only about half-an-hour away. Our American rower will snowboard (this seems wild). We join a small mid-week crowd at the ski-hire hut. It's all new for me. The normal approach would be to have a group lesson or splash out on a private, but this doesn't occur to us here for the day only. The hire staff size us up for ski-length.

"Beginner," I state, gamely, for the record.

Richard puffs out his chest, and proudly claims:

"Intermediate."

The hire guys look at me and suck in through their teeth, gauging my weight. Boot sizes are in Euro specs, so I check fit perched on a wooden bench surrounded by other punters, adults and kids. There's the slight aroma of sweaty socks in the air. I'm careful to avoid the pools of melted snow on the floor. Richard explains how to click-in to the ski bindings, toe in first, then heel, and we are set for my inaugural ski.

We shuffle to the tow.

"Okay, watch me, I'll go first," he calls.

He waits for the next lift to come around, and it collects him and drags him up the slope. I stand in what I understand is the correct spot, and soon I'm following behind, much to my satisfaction. It's okay for several hundred metres untiI I hit a mound in the snow which catches me off guard, and I skid off helplessly whilst the conga line of professionals serenely climbs to the summit without me. Richard has noticed:

"Steve, see you at the top!" he shouts.

I register his receding back and can only guess he's relieved to be no longer responsible for me.

I find myself half-way up the top of a run in a natural saddle, with no place to go. It dawns on me what goes up, must come down in this line of play.

*Got to get down. What did Richard say about the technique?*

I start my run, a sickening feeling in my stomach, and not sure how to turn, which will slow me down. The theory does not translate to the practice. It's no surprise I progress from "slow to go" in seconds. It's a miracle I don't hit anyone, and when I've picked up a bit of speed, I decide I've had enough—but now I'm worried. Balancing, and staying upright, is in fact a breeze. It's the stopping that is the new challenge. The answer occurs to me. I'll throw myself to the ground.

It's solves the issue, but cold snow soaks through my trousers and up the back of my top as I lie a quarter up the piste.

*Great.*

So, I ski using this technique after all, and manage to occupy myself for a couple of hours.

When we rendezvous back at the ski hire, we find we are burnt to a crisp. Richard, particularly, has white panda eyes from his large Bolle sunglasses, but Mr American still looks like the ultimate dude, having enjoyed his snowboard. But, as we discover when we get back, most of the club have also been burnt by the spring rays, fooled by the cool days and altitude. We titter despite the soreness. Still, there is a chance to cheer up; we reckon most of us have the finances to stretch to a meal. We head out to a local pizzeria diner, and it's there we establish Switzerland isn't exactly the cheap destination of choice.

"What are you having, Richard?" someone says.

"Caesar salad with Chicken," he says, slamming his menu

closed and throwing it on the table.

"Have you seen the price, though?"

He runs his finger down the menu again.

"On second thoughts, I'll get the Carbonara."

The drinks list gets passed around too, and there's a sucking in of air and laughter.

"Let's have the one drink and sneak back to the hostel," someone says.

# 22 THE RUNNING OF THE BULLS

S pring is now firmly established. The days are getting longer and longer. There's an uptick in London life as the capital awakes. Patrons in bars and cafes spill out on to the pavement. There are consecutive days of glorious sunshine, and people sit out in Green Park, and boat-hire on the Serpentine is doing a brisk business. In the words of Tennyson: *In the Spring a fuller crimson comes upon the robin's breast...In the Spring a young man's fancy lightly turns to thoughts of love.*

And Rachael and I are getting along fine, enjoying the lengthening days and warmer weather. Also, the trip down there is that much easier in daylight and without fog.

Before summer gets a chance to take hold, though, I am settled down with a book which outlines how Foreign Exchange rates work. Of competing interest is a packet of Monster Munch I am grazing on, and a cup of tea with sugar and milk, hot and steaming on the coffee table in front of the TV.

My mobile rings, and for a moment, I wonder who could be calling me at that late time. Not everyone has one, and past a certain time it's rare to get a call from anyone. It's from Pete, a mate who is a few years older than me. He left for the US, chasing the love of his life. He's had the good fortune to study on the East coast, doing a Masters at Massachusetts Institute of Technology in Cambridge. (It's just across the Charles River in Boston.)

Not only is he living it up in Boston, he's joined their rugby team. It's not a big sport over there, but there is a following at collegiate level, and the US plans to send the Eagles to the 1999 Rugby World Cup. The team is keen as mustard, and have cottoned on to the fact a key point of the game is go on tour and enjoy themselves.

Their destination of choice—to tour Spain—and, given they haven't got enough players to form a squad, they are putting out feelers for additional players. Pete wants to know if I can make it.

"It'll be great Steve, get yourself over to Madrid on the 24th. Left Wing, Right Wing, or Outside Centre, right?"

*This looks great.*

"Right mate, let me check the schedule."

I have a moment of hesitation.

*Now come on Steve, you need to be studying and there are the seminars that week.*

I check my diary—I can definitely skip lectures that week.

"I'm in mate," I confirm.

*Happy Days.*

The Airbus lands in Madrid, which I've only ever shot through on the train before, years back, when I took the Interrail trip. It doesn't take long to transfer to the station, working out the signs in Spanish from what I know from French as I go. I scan the departures board for the train heading for a town that matches my itinerary.

Our first game on tour starts right after we get in—there's not much of a margin. On the platform, I discover I've missed the train by minutes. The guard tells me in broken English there's another one in an hour, so I can follow on behind the rest of the team. The train trundles through the suburbs of Madrid, and I stand by the map following all the little station halts. I have a mobile number I can call when I get there, but a girl is waiting for me with a SEAT hot hatch. She gives me a little wave,

"Steve?"

I smile broadly, and we chuck my bag in the back and scoot off to the fixture.

I arrive at the pitch to find it's half-time, and the team is switching out subs and taking stock of tactics. The score is 9-18 in their favour. Pete looks over and nods,

"Steve, you're on in ten for the second half. Left wing."

*My preference.*

I locate my gear in my backpack and change on the side of the pitch, lacing my boots up. I don't have a top, so a player being subbed chucks me his muddy jersey. There's no time to stretch and warm up, or talk plays, before the whistle goes, and it's not long before I find myself near our touch line at a scrum feed, our put in.

Pete playing blindside flanker—Number Six—drives over the ball, picks it up, pops it to me and I break for the line, getting tackled by the opposition flanker. Ten minutes later, our hooker goes off with a broken finger, and 30 minutes later, we've lost the game. The ball got bogged down in the forwards, so I've barely broken a sweat. There are slaps on the backs, and smiles all around from our hosts after their deserved win.

"We were simply outclassed," one of my new teammates says, "I'm Jason, by the way."

He's wearing scrum-half, number nine.

No one on the team can disagree. On the other hand, no one could say they were that bothered either.

After a hot shower, and changed, we stand in the rooms and I am introduced, and our secretary throws over my Number 11 tour top which I catch. Most of the team are budding engineers and technologists, barely out of their teens, and are great company. Our touring captain is Jason, and we also have an events secretary, Oscar, from the United States Marines Officer Reserve Training corps, with a "high and tight" crew cut, who prefers to play Inside Centre, but can play Outside Centre at a pinch. There's a wafer-thin Winger of Dutch ancestry with blond hair who looks like he has to run around in circles in the shower to get wet. Our hooker won't be playing any more games this tour and will sit it out on the sideline.

The next day, we bus it down to Pamplona for the next game. Us backs run through drills on the pitch, and I get to work with my Outside Centre and Full Back. There's a possibility we can do a "scissor" move, and I can come in-field, we'll see. I stretch, sprint at 80 per cent pace, this is not a time to get injured —and get ready for kick-off. The mouthguard goes in last, I remembered to pack it. We win the toss and choose to kick with the wind. However, the opposition are a good team—maybe too good a team for us. I injure my hand in a tackle. We lose the game.

A sister of one of the teammates from the team we were playing takes us on our own private tour around downtown, through sun-dappled streets under azure skies.

The town is best known for the world-renowned "Running of the Bulls"—Feast of San Fermín—held in July every year. We hear about how the bulls are released and pursue dare-devil runners who have nowhere to go. Many are plucked to safety by the crowd lining the streets, or make it over barricades or into alleyways, or scale drainpipes in their haste to avoid a goring by the stampede.

"Who would fancy it?" Jason asks.

There's a consensus some of our number would love to give it a go, but the tour will have ended by then.

We visit Hemingway's bar where the great raconteur himself drank in his afternoons—when he wasn't writing *The Sun Also Rises*, presumably, or needed inspiration. We buy large glasses of beer and occupy most of the tables near the bar. The younger boys down these drinks perhaps faster than strictly necessary, and a few fellows break open a deck of cards for poker.

In a pleasing early evening, a family hosts us at a dairy farm on the outskirts of the city and we bus it down there to find tables and trestles lined up in a spare barn.

We can't believe our luck—we sit down, and before we know it, family members are carrying in bread baskets and large pots of soup for our entrée. Bottles of beer and cider are on offer, and it's not long before we are in a rambunctious mood, every man an emperor. Our hosts lift main courses in on huge trays; beef, chicken and lamb. They are passed over our heads and set down amongst a hungry team needing sustenance. The team captains make speeches, and our Spanish families beam, but most of us haven't got a clue what is being said. We lost the game, on one hand, but scored on the hospitality and bonhomie on the other.

The Spaniards love the nightlife, and our hosts take us out to nightspots late at night. There's a venue in a cavernous warehouse next to a vineyard and we meet the friends of our hosts.

In our next town on the tour, we have taken over the entire top floor of two youth hostels opposite each other in the old centre. We spill out on to the balconies, calling across, and look down at the cobbled flags of the old town.

"Hey Dude, look down there," intones an American voice.

The team roams from room to room inspecting each other's digs.

Here, the trip does take a serious turn, other than yet another loss. Oscar doesn't know when to ease up or keep quiet. He has one too many and doesn't take it well when he earns the attention of the bouncers at a venue. What starts as a sneer and backchat escalates suddenly. They decide he's had enough, and they bundle him out into the street. He's got the measure of a bouncer; a few punches are thrown, but when help arrives, he is outnumbered and next thing, he's in a headlock.

We only find out this story when Jason makes the trip to the hospital in the small hours with the local police to collect him. He asks Pete and me if we can join him down there, as older teammates. The police have decided not to place charges, and there's a call to the United States Embassy. After a checkup, Oscar is repatriated to our accommodation with a bit of concussion, bloodshot eyes and, whilst bruised and quieter, still arrogant, thinking he did nothing wrong.

"Those bouncers had it coming to them," he snarls aggressively.

The next night he's still grandstanding, muscling in on teammates when they talk to the local girls—he's a bully. I tell him to give it a rest, and he runs a hand through my hair patronisingly.

"Yeah, Limey!"

We play in Barcelona—and lose again, before turning our attention once more to a city where again the nightlife is king. We explore the harbour, and the seafood restaurants, and fill up on paella and calamari in the dazzling Spanish light, tasting the Spanish ales. The seafood is freshly cooked, the fillets lush, the calamari crispy and freshly sourced from the Med. We promenade down the main avenue, loving it, looking at the shops.

Sure, we weren't able to make our mark as a touring side, but boy, did we care, we couldn't have been happier. And my hand was as right as rain within weeks.

*** 

Rachel and I are downstairs in her sitting room lying on the sofa having just got out of bed. She's pulled on a t-shirt, and sunshine comes in through the thin glaze of the windows, from the garden. The flowers are going gangbusters in the warmth, and bees circulate from one opportunity to another. I can't help but admire the curve of her hip, and her sturdy legs, and how straight and particular her thighs are, and I tell her so. She giggles. The conversation turns to Spain.

"I wish I had come with you," she says. "You're a winger? That's the one that runs down the sides?"

I laugh at the impression she has got.

"Yeah, then get tackled most of the time."

Rachael marvelled at our audacity and spirit, but wasn't so impressed with our American ambassador. She gets up to make another cup of tea.

"He sounds horrible!" she says.

## 23 NOTHING EXTRA

Time to buckle down to final essays, and consider the lead up to exams once essays are turned in. But my mind is still on other opportunities, but perhaps for good reason. A friend, Tom, had been telling us about his work in his latest film, *First Knight*, with Richard Gere, Sean Connery and Ben Cross. He had landed the role of Assistant Swordmaster. He rings me and tells me to get down to the set at Pinewood.

A lot of men in my infantry company got film work over the years. One bloke got a role in *Batman*, a speaking part as a croupier. He also had a close-up shot in *Full Metal Jacket*, firing an anti-tank missile—and had worked as an archer in *Henry V*. Others had played Nazis in *Indiana Jones and the Last Crusade*. I call a friend, and we catch the train together. We meet Tom and the casting lead in the Production Office.

"It's 60 pounds a day, guys, and we'll send you a cheque after filming," the lead says.

To a student, this seems like unfathomable riches. When I phone Rachael, flushed with excitement, she reckons this is a bad idea,

"You need to be focusing on those exams coming up, not off for a week or two," she says.

I believe I can swing it, though, and tell her so. I forget I have little wiggle room after failing an exam earlier in the year.

"And, what happens if you fail another exam, you'll have to retake it?"

"Let's not fret about that, it might never happen," I reply.

On the outdoor lot, the studio has built a gigantic fibreglass golden castle, representing Camelot. When we see men and women preparing horses outside the castle gates, I get chatting with them during our lunch break. They are on the princely sum of 120 pounds a day. I should have got in sooner when the call to arms went out.

In one scene, Malagant attacks Camelot interrupting a trial where Sean Connery (King Arthur) challenges Richard Gere (Sir Lancelot). Malagant's knights race on horseback into the courtyard through the archway, his foot soldiers surrounding the Royal Guards. Malagant makes a speech to the people, and King Arthur is about to kneel before him. He leaps up, and shouts for his court to "fight and never surrender."

The effects guys have organised a volley of arrows to strike him in the chest. That's the signal for us to clash with swords.

For some shots, we assemble off the lot outside, and are marshalled and placed on call by a crewmember with a walkie-talkie who relays to us from someone co-ordinating the shot from below. We hear:

"Rolling...Sound...Lights...and—ACTION!"

He sees a signal, then nods to us to swarm through a doorway.

There's a fair amount of time in between takes, and we chat on the castle battlements. There are lots of Australians and New Zealanders, with their slow drawls and rising inflexion sentences (people from Sydney) or clipped vowels (Aucklanders, or Wellington people). We have a chance to bond and laugh, watching the crew prepare the set. Sean Connery, Richard Gere and Julia Ormond stand in their positions before each take, and lighting people scurry around checking reflective screens. That's if they can get around the makeup people making small touch-ups to these principals.

It is cold out there, without our jackets, but we are so pleased to be filming a major film we couldn't have cared less.

There seems to be a pecking order on set. The Hollywood principals need no introduction, but there are also some "blow-ins" from British TV looking pleased to be there. There's a bloke from the cop show *The Bill*—whose name escapes me—and minor acting royalty. Later down the batting order are various stuntmen followed by us, a motley crew of extras. A few of the fighting stuntmen are riders, and they command three times our daily rate. I rue momentarily with better organisation and warning, I could have had a go, but riding in armour and with weaponry is no mean feat.

In fact, there's a pecking order in the extras. Some are positioned close to the camera and seem to know exactly how to carry themselves, with a certain glance or look at the right time. Possibly stage-school kids, rather good-looking too, we concede —we can't tell. We are at the bottom of the pile, but content to be there at all. None of us have any formal training, but I had received sword instruction in thrusting, forward strokes, and parrying, which I figure I can reuse.

We are being paid, but we are also fed lunch and snacks from vans set up outside the castle. Sean and Richard are nowhere to be seen during any break longer than a few minutes, hiding away in their trailers. Sean is whisked out of sight at any opportunity, but Richard is happy to chat even when he returns to find me sitting in his chair. The camera men and lighting consult intently between shots and re-arrange big umbrellas as the light changes, like cricket groundsmen moving screens around.

Many of the takes are lengthy, and we shoot lots to bag the shots a certain director, Mr Zucker, wants. At one point, the set is set on fire for realism. For some scenes, track is placed down quickly for the camera to track up and down for as many takes as necessary, then taken back up just as fast during a break. Rumours fly around about Richard Gere and Cindy Crawford, but our instructions are to say nothing and not talk to the press.

*** 

After playing the part of a marauder, I am offered a change of costume to play a villager—a "good guy". I am now wearing a dyed orange medieval tunic down to my thighs and a grey shawl around my neck, tights and a cool pair of boots.

A close-up is scheduled with Ben Cross and Richard Gere, requiring stuntmen and extras fighting in the background. Tom had been discussing the shot with the Assistant Director and asked him whether he could use a "few more blokes", so he calls me over.

I find a better sword in the props trolley, and we rehearse a sequence of moves I can reproduce.

"Right, Steve," he says, "this is my sword, watch this."

He demonstrates moves—lunging forward to attack, stepping back neatly to defend.

"You'll be in shot, if–you stand here." He indicates it with a foot he plants down on set. "Good luck."

He's busy though, with other plays, so he doesn't hang around for long. My friend is also intimately involved in another shot on the other side of the set and is enjoying himself immensely. Reunited at a meal break, we compare notes about our scenes and make a note of what to look for in the movie when we see it.

On the train returning from Iver back to London, we must look a proper sight—with our foundation and screen makeup, we resemble drag queens.

## 24 TRAIN HARD, FIGHT EASY

I'm surprised when my stepfather rings me asking me whether I'll join him for a trip on the Norfolk Broads. He has hired a small dinghy, and is taking a quick break from his parish. I agree to meet to spend the day with him. He meets me at Norfolk station with his 1980 W registration navy Volvo, minus his clerical collar and dressed in a twill shirt, blue vee-necked jumper and characteristic cords. His trousers are slightly too short, exposing his socks.

After our day out, he takes me for a drink at a choice pub on the waterfront. He's worked out this is by far the best he has found so far on his trip—he's done his reconnaissance.

"Two pints of bitter, please," he asks the barmaid—patrons glance up—"and a packet of peanuts," he adds, almost *sotte voce*.

We take them outside into the evening sun to a bench which we straddle.

"How's Rachael?" he asks.

"Good."

"I've got a message from your mother," he announces. "How's the degree course going? And have you got any plans for next year? Been a while since we caught up."

I tell him as far as I know, I'll get through exams, and I've got a job next year lined up. This is true—there's a job opportunity for me waiting regardless of results. It's a role with the Army—an office job, but a job. I was able to swing this via contacts in London.

"Good, your mother will be pleased. I'll let her know."

We stop talking and look at a dinghy coming past down the water.

"Good luck in your finals," he adds.

And we drink to it.

***

At Rachael's, I take over the kitchen table and spread my books out. I read my notes, and skim through the texts—I'm quietly confident. I rue that money is still tight, but I'm aware if I complete enough military training that is coming up after exams, I'll get the tax-free bonus from the Ministry of Defence. I need the substantial cash prize to help pay down my loan. Two goals, one after the other. Rachael is off in town looking at horse supplies, but comes back for dinner which we enjoy in the garden looking over the hills.

In London, I sit the exams, three hours in each session. There's enough timetabled to stretch us. It feels like a marathon, not a sprint, but I feel I've done well enough in them. No panics. I pack to go away, a backpack and a duffle bag, then I call Rachael.

"I'll see you when I get back, I'll be out of mobile range for most of it, and I won't be able to get to a phone, OK?"

"Take care," she says.

The training is in Dundee, Scotland. The entire battalion has travelled up from all parts of the south ahead of me while I was taking my last exam.

The route back up north is the same as earlier in the year —by train—but I am picked up by a camouflaged Land Rover at the station by the duty driver from the guardroom. He is a handsome man, who, knowing he will be out in public on display, has taken a bit more care over ironing in creases into his tropical shirt, and consideration into how he has cuffed his trousers over his buffed boots.

It's glorious north of the border, approaching midsummer's day, the solstice.

*The druids will be heading down to Stonehenge.*

The training is a machine gun course, which teaches us how to mount a gun on a tripod and locate, and fire on targets in support of closing infantry. The gun puts down lunatic rates of fire to suppress positions we would be attacking. It would be terrifying for soldiers on the receiving end. We can shoot out accurately to over a mile, which is an impressive feat. So we can see where we are aiming, we have the option of staking a reference sight into the ground, so that the gun's aim can be returned to the same position at night, and, still find the target.

There's classroom work where the platoon commander, a lieutenant, explains how bullets trace arcs in the air before landing on target. Bullets disperse in a "cone of fire" and when they land on the ground, it's called a "beaten zone" to trap the unwary.

One morning, I don't shave as close as I should, and someone notices.

"Steve. You need to watch yourself, mate, the 'Razzman' is around."

The Regimental Sergeant Major (RSM) is the senior soldier in the battalion—he is, if not literally, a god appointed over us and sits at the right hand of the Commanding Officer, a lieutenant colonel. To my dismay, I see him strutting around the corner, his badge of rank worn on his wrist. Luckily, he doesn't spot anything amiss, and at break, I fish out my razor from my locker and make amends. He could have jailed me in the guardroom for a few hours.

We need to be fit to carry the gun and ammunition. Each platoon in the company has the racing snakes, the guys who leave the rest of us well behind in gym gear. Then there are the blokes who carry a bit of weight, which sort of helps for the loaded runs, and even the platoon smokers who despite their self-imposed handicap are still good for the course.

Midweek, there's Physical Training (PT). We stand outside the block getting ready for a loaded run. Thankfully, this won't be with packs (overnight gear, spare clothing, or radio batteries), only the weight of the "guns" themselves and "belt order". This is the harness that carries water, rations, medical kit, and the basics to fight in the field.

I roll up the sleeves of the jungle shirt I am wearing, and stretch out my calves and hamstrings. I cinch up my boot laces.

I take the machine gun, one bloke shoulders the tripod, and Dan takes his rifle and some ammunition link—five hundred rounds weighs thirteen kilogrammes. We will rotate these loadings around as we run.

After an hour, the sun is climbing in the sky and the dew on the grass tops is drying out. Our boots kick up dirt from the track and then sand, as we head out towards a dune scape. It's not hot, this is Scotland, but it's still mid-summer, and I am glad we are not wearing smocks.

The instructors have asked us to climb the first dune and loop back—they are not looking to kill us before lunch. Dan with his ammunition leads the way with me in the middle, and he breaks into an exaggerated walk, breathing in through his nose and out through his mouth and swinging his rifle. We sink our efforts into getting there. Dan stops unselfishly before the brow for us all to join him, and we walk the final steps to the top.

## 25 IN TO THE WILD

Two girls lounge on beach towels, both with a leg drawn-up, opposite legs, enjoying the warm weather. They are wearing skimpy bikinis. One has large breasts, flatted by gravity, and brings her hand up to her face to swat away a fly. She has a flat stomach and an oval-shaped navel and raven brown hair. Her friend is blonde and slimmer and turns on to her front. Her buttocks shimmy as she comes about and takes her weight on her folded arms, face tilted up into the sun.

The girl who has turned over gasps.

I remove my cap to appear friendly.

"Hi Girls," I say lamely, but also running a hand through my hair.

The girl lying on her back sits up bolt-upright and hoists her beach bag on to her lap to shield herself.

"Hi," she says awkwardly.

We wipe our brows. I sling the machine gun over my shoulder, shrugging it over to my back, keeping my arm crooked to support the weight. Dan drops his left hand off his rifle foregrip and allows the weapon to hang non-aggressively in his right. We try to look nonchalant, friendly, and never one to lose an opportunity to chat up pretty girls, Dan goes into bat.

"Sorry, girls, didn't want to scare you, we are on a navigation exercise, a bit of training really," he says.

"That's ok," says one.

"Are you English?" the other asks, hearing the accent.

"Yeah, London," Dan agrees.

*Hopefully they won't label us as typical Sassenachs (Englishmen).*

I can see Dan is turning on the charm by degrees.

"Are you Army?" asks one of the girls.

Never mind the fact we are dressed in green and tooled up.

"Yeah, Parachute Regiment," Dan says, making sure he gets that in quick. We're an elite, remember?

"What, like parachuting?" one asks.

"Yes," confirms Dan. It's not necessarily a silly question, it's a typical response we've noticed over the years.

"Have those guns got bullets?" asked the other.

"No," I say, "that's not allowed."

There's a bit of small talk.

"What are you girls doing later," Dan asks. "Want to meet up?"

The girls look at each other, and there's body-language and glances of the sort which only girls can decipher.

"Sure, we are in town later this week."

"Great, we can get the evening off," Dan says.

The girl with the beach bag gets a pen and writes a number down on a page torn from her diary.

***

Dan unlocks the machine gun cradle and shifts the barrel to point to our next target 1,600 metres away.

*That's a mile.*

"Lay!" I shout.

"On," he calls, locking the gun and checking he's aligned with the reference post.

"Fire!" I call.

A stream of rounds spit from the barrel, in a cone shape, as it happens. As we have added tracer rounds, one in five, we can see them describe a lazy, loping trajectory out to the target. It's surreal and not like anything you'd see in a movie. At night, it's even beautiful.

Seeing we are on, I say:

"No need to adjust," I murmur.

I can see the rounds land on target in a beaten zone and give him the thumbs up and smile.

Our satisfaction is soon interrupted by a distant puff of smoke when we see the gorse has caught alight: it's not hot, but the vegetation has dried out by even a Scottish June day. There is no other option than to jog almost two kilometres out with mops to put out the fire. And the same back, of course. So, a simple day turns out to be more physical than anticipated.

After puffing through the terrain with the gear we need, we arrive at the edge of the fire front, and swat like French peasants, bending from the waist laboriously, sucking in air as we rise. Like bush firefighters, we start with the edges and flanks of the small blaze. Smaller spots, sort of little islands smouldering, are tackled later as we get to them. Satisfied, we jog back.

We are breathing hard, and have a well-earned cup of tea from a Thermos container. There are, however, other challenges and dramas to come. When we traverse our barrel on to our final lay point, we notice sheep have departed from their flock and have roamed over towards our field of fire.

"Cease fire Cease fire!" Dan bellows in my ear.

I apply my safety catch, lower the butt to the ground and peer downrange, laughing, squinting down the sights.

"Just think of the compensation those farmers would have got," he says.

*Maybe we will get a commission.*

***

The back end of the week, we patrol out into the terrain around Garelochhead, near where I had sailed out from previously. The countryside has a wilderness feel to it, deeper glades and forested areas. It is stunningly beautiful, and I recall—again— the old observation that truly, Scotland would be the answer to your holiday dreams if only the weather was better. But it's not the weather now that is a problem.

When dusk arrives, we find a new nuisance. The Scots midge makes an appearance in the tens of thousands, looking to bite. These are not the larger mossies you see in foreign climes, but the tiny ones you can barely see, heralded by a small whine. With nowhere to go, they make our lives a misery. We roam the harbour area with cam netting shawls over our faces, with only eyes showing, so it's hard to see who's who. By week's end, we have mottled and bruised faces from the incessant attacks.

My section commander needs to check "nav"—and can't be sure where we are (a euphemism for getting lost) and calls a halt for half an hour on a section of forest that descends to the water. It's a welcome reprieve from the exertion.

We are in light order, fighting order—water, ammunition, bit of medical kit, rations. Our snacks are scattered throughout our pockets to be found one by one, and the melted chocolate Rolos hurt our teeth when bits of foil touch fillings. Sweat drips down to the small of our backs. One soldiering luxury is dropping our trousers to our knees, re-arranging our underwear, and shifting a belt into a more sustainable position. The war movies don't show the soddenness, the sweat, the load-carrying, and the faff of it all.

"Get a brew on Steve," he asks civilly.

He extracts his map from a thigh pocket and goes into quiet conference with the second-in-command. The radio-operator squats nearby with his signal codebooks. He's grateful when I pass up a large mug of hot tea, made with a packet of dry milk and sugar sachets.

We cruise open waterways and inlets in fast raiding boats, disembarking quickly, water up to our knees, our rifles above our heads. The wind coming off the water makes my teeth chatter, and the shoreline approaching is welcome. We squelch around the countryside, and it's a blessing to stop and drain the water out of our boots and wring out socks when we halt for more than fifteen minutes. The old sweats have a string across their shoulders from jacket, armpit to armpit, to hang their socks— body heat finishing the job. Dry socks are a luxury for sleeping.

We locate the enemy and put in attacks against embedded troops, firing and advancing in pairs in the heather before posting a grenade. Often, they peel away into the terrain behind their lines, and we are no closer to flushing them out. In the quieter periods, lying in the grass with sweat running in to my eyes, I think back to the way Rachael looks naked before it's time to get to my feet again.

## 26 CONFLICT

An obliging non-commissioned officer (NCO) gives some of the platoon including myself and Dan a lift down to the local village pub and we stroll in, wearing fleeces, desert boots and sweatshirts, the 1990s "walk-out" dress for the military. Do we look like the local Royal Navy on a night out? Will we fit in? The platoon starts with drinks in the saloon, enjoying the local beer, or lagers, being eyed up by locals. Our leadership group, a few captains, a lieutenant and warrant officers leave early for dinner, dressed in waxed Barbours in gloss or matte lustre depending on age. Sailors from the subbase nearby are also here, and some stop by and say "Hello."

Dan says:

"Let's sit in the beer garden."

*Good idea.*

With our jugs, we find a spare table. In the summer evening, the light dapples from the established trees above.

There is a gaggle of girls on a few tables nearby, and we glance at them in between taking sips of bitter or lager, and in between small talk. Some of them glance back; they obviously don't recognise us as locals. Have they guessed we are "military"?

Nearing chuck-out time, 11 pm, we get our last rounds in. By now we are relaxed, and there is more mingling inside, and in neutral territory at the bar, and in a 'no-man's-land' next to a dance floor. It's still empty.

Dan gets a call, and it's from the girls we met in the dunes wanting to catch up before we head out of town.

"We're heading back to London, Thursday," he says. "We're in the King's Arms till late."

"We'll see you down there, just getting ready," one replies.

They arrive not long after, in tank tops and high-waisted denim jeans, giggling, and ask for a Southern Comfort. It's hard to remember through an alcohol-riddled haze, but later, Dan and I find ourselves outside the pub with one of them. There's another girl from town, who lives around the corner and is amused to see a bunch of new boys in her local.

She tells me it's her birthday, so we sit down on a bench. We are a little befuddled by drink. I'm tight as hell; I've had way more than I planned. Dan is feeling amorous—this is his chance and he disappears with his girl, probably for a kiss. The birthday girl leans in closer, and says, almost shyly, but in a matter-of-fact way,

"You're really cute. I'll snog you later."

"Hey, I've got a girlfriend, you know," I say.

"Really…" she replies.

In the early hours of the morning, I leave a nightclub doing brisk business for a breath of fresh air. I look up at the twilight still visible in the sky on this midsummer's night, this far north. It will only be truly dark for a few hours. I decide to buy a kebab and take a shortcut through a carpark behind a supermarket, walking past a group of locals. As I round a corner into a darker part of the carpark, one man breaks off and approaches, suddenly threatening.

"Come here!" he shouts.

I choose a line that takes me away from him, but he increases his pace.

"Give me your money!" he drawls in a local brogue.

The others gather around and leer. I stand my ground, refuse, and turn. One of the guys lunges forward. The rest close in. I decide, there and then.

Offence is the best defence: I'll strike first.

I go in, arms wheeling—surely aggression and surprise, are the watchwords here. I land accurate blows to the head of the first bloke, the ringleader, figuring if I can put him off, the gang will lose interest—a timeless strategy. Through a sea of blows coming back my way, I connect with jaws and foreheads. I am surrounded, but I can tell I have landed accurate hits. Sensing I am getting the upper hand, I get some precise jabs in. One reels away, clutching a bloody nose.

"Let's go guys!" one shouts, and they scarper. It's not worth the hassle.

I turn the corner, and by sheer chance, a police car crawls up with two policemen.

I don't want to draw attention to myself, but the constable who leads with the questioning wants to know what is going on. He's heard the scuffle and seen the gang flee. I tell him. Even more carelessly, I explain I'm with the military on the Clyde.

"Regiment?" the other asks.

"Parachute Regiment," I say.

They exchange knowing glances, and take me back to the police station for a statement. I insist I am fine, that there's nothing to see here. Things turn sour when they think I need to get checked out, so take me to the Royal Navy base hospital, which I reckon is a waste of time, mine and theirs. I'm quite certain a painkiller and a band aid, and a night's sleep will suffice and see me on my way. The Royal Navy doctor at Faslane is rather snotty and I'm tired, sore and irksome by now.

"Name," the officer enquires superciliously.

"Malins," I reply.

"Sir, what about Sir?" he counters.

*Who do you think you are?*

"I'm a soldier in the Parachute Regiment and Airborne Forces," I say, and I allow myself an impudent grin.

The implication is he does not register. My line is one we are encouraged to use mischievously when out and about. This irritates him somewhat, and he strides off in a huff.

Still, the nurse rating is now a lot sweeter, and gently swabs at my bruises—it looks like there is no damage here after all. The duty NCO who is turned out of bed in the early hours is not happy when he arrives in a four-tonne truck to pick me up. He grumbles all the way back on the side roads to barracks, making hard work of shifting the gears.

\*\*\*

Paratroopers are renowned for their aggression, which the regiment rather relies on in wartime in the hope any enemy force will give up and surrender before committing to battle—this reputation also spills over into fighting amongst themselves. On the return from the Falklands War, a brawl broke out on the requisitioned North Sea ferry MV Norland as returning paras from the second battalion got drunk and fought with each other.

As I am not in my platoon, let alone company—the first largish unit of allegiance in a battalion—when news of my escapade filters out, I am not popular for getting ambushed in the way I did. Although nothing has been said, I'm also the "middle-class boy" amongst a crew of "harder" south-Londoners, many who have perhaps said nothing, but now have a reason to find me suspect.

The NCO who had to pick me up stirs trouble. The next night, I am confined to barracks as punishment, and am dozing in the quiet and solitude of the room whilst my section is out in town. There are about 15 beds, not enough for our platoon, so the overflow is next door.

I wake up to find a member of the platoon needing to relieve himself, standing over me. I sit up in bed and push him away. He squares up to me and I can see he's had a skinful. I think he wants to take payment for the slight to the regiment's reputation.

*Here we go.*

One of the blokes decides we should sort this out between us, and there is no time like the present. One distinct matter will decide, or factor into a win, loss, or draw. My opponent is drunk, skin flushed, eyes open, but dulled. I am not. A section commander gives us special dispensation to cover our fists with scraps of foam rubber.

Someone, keen as a spectator, volunteers this from his field sleeping mat, even if it means he'll sleep less well outside in the nights to come when he is sober.

We face each other sullenly, not with hatred, with focus and resolve: just two young men from an infantry platoon. What's more, I can't say I am a pugilist, but that's immaterial now. A junior NCO acting as umpire cues us off:

"FIGHT!"

I move in quick, wanting to get the "knockout" blows in first.

This is a good idea, as perhaps my opponent hasn't considered his alcohol-riddled brain and overconfidence, Dutch or otherwise. My fists connect in a fusillade of strikes. He falters backwards and goes down. I back off, catching my breath, making sure I don't take my eye off him. He's taken a knock and blood oozes from a cut on his forehead. The foam has slipped, so now we are down to bare knuckles.

Our umpire resets us, and we go again. I think my opponent regrets his aggression, and the spectators seem satisfied for the time being.

"That's it, lads. OK, you've sorted it," comes an older voice.

I slip back between the sheets knowing sleep will come soon.

The next morning, we settle, shaking hands, and I feel in some way I have regained any sort of prestige or reputation I may have lost. The rest of the platoon grin at me, and my opponent is subdued. I reflect briefly on the trials and tribulations of a young man in a rough environment—and decide to chalk it up to life experience.

## 27 FOR THE CHOP

I'm thinking of Rachael, looking forward to seeing her, but there's not too much time, as our helicopter arrives and comes into land to lift us to our next position.

"Stand by!" shouts our section commander.

He raises his arms above his head to guide the pilot in, we wait in-line safely out of the rotating blades. We jog to the door, heads well down. One of my section has a shovel at the top of his pack, which comes loose and smacks his head.

"It got me," he told us later, probably wondering if they were his last thoughts.

In Hollywood movies, there is plenty of room for the grinning squad, and space for a gunner in the door too. The Army Air Corps have provided us with Westland Scouts, but they don't fit many. Some of us will need to wait for the next lift.

I am last in with the bulky machine gun. With our gear and spare ammunition links, there is not enough room for me. I back up and sit in the doorway and my oppo places his arm around my waist. For additional security, my feet can just about reach the skids. There's no time to agonise, because someone gives the loadmaster the thumbs up, and we sour away.

We fly nap of the earth to remain undetected, and the hills and valleys contour past us. I zone out and put the danger out of mind. For a startling moment, one of my boots slips on the skids, and I lurch briefly, but the security of that arm keeps me in place. It's a relief, though, to get down on *terra firma*.

Later, we abseil from the helicopters, a way of getting down fast.

This wasn't new for me. I used to go abseiling with mates in a stone quarry near Box Hill on the North Downs outside London. It was only a few hours hike to the location, through woodlands, mostly deserted. It was where they filmed the planet scenes of the 1970s TV space series *Blake's 7*. We'd run a rope around a tree as anchor but didn't use a secondary rope. Those were the days, too, before people wore helmets. We ran the risks.

So, with gear and slung rifle, in pairs, it's a breeze, "stopping no stations" all the way down. We need to step off simultaneously, so the pilot can keep the helicopter level. Dan drops too soon, and the helicopter tilts alarmingly towards the ground until the pilot can correct with a deft hand on the controls. We have a laugh about it later.

*** 

I head out west to see Rachael armed with bad news. When I got back to London, I discovered to my chagrin I had failed my Employment Law exam. The result was staring up at me from a typed sheet of A4, folded in to three, that had arrived in the post.

*Great*. The omen is not a good one, I will have to retake the exam in order to graduate. As I had the chance to rue, I had used up my last life earlier in the year.

I sit in the little kitchen with a cup of tea and Rachel sits opposite in a cable-knit jumper with a concerned look on her face.

"So, I dropped a subject–failed one," I say. Rachael replies,

"What are you going to do? I warned you about this, Steve."

"Rachael, this is not a headache. I can retake in the early autumn before graduation."

I'm confident I can pull this off, if I put my mind to it. I've only got one subject to put all my energies into. She leans closer and inspects the damage to my nose.

"Let's have another look," she gets up close and examines it.

"There might be a slight break, there Steve," she murmurs.

Perhaps the cartilage is visible after all, it's hard to say. I've been too busy to really look. What did it look like before? I wonder.

"You *boys*," she says finally, with a bit of consternation. She looks worried.

"What kind of company do you keep?"

I suppose, as a matter of fact, it is open to debate: my mother has asked the same question. We head out the door for a walk around town, and she is a bit distant.

## 28 NINE AND A HALF WEEKS

The tennis—Wimbledon—comes and goes, no British success there as always; the weather improves. My aim is still to take up a small role full-time with the Army at the main HQ for UK forces in early 1996. This gives me the clear path to sail at the end of the year.

Retaking the exam in the autumn, and then sailing, was not entirely on my mind—I had prior commitments. Last year, before I had decided to head out to the Caribbean, I had arranged nine and a half weeks (I'm reminded of the movie and Kim Basinger) in the United States, destination—a children's summer camp in New York state. This isn't Camp America—this is the more jocular Camp Counsellors USA. Once they discover I have a sailing qualification, they decide I can help on the lake with their jet skis. It's water, I suppose.

I discussed it with Rachael, at the start of the year, when I outlined my commitments, and she was ok with the idea then, but now once more laments me being away now the plan is about to become a reality.

"It's ok, I am going to be busy with a hotel opening then anyhow."

I present her with a stack of blue pre-paid Royal Mail aerogrammes, and we agree to write regularly.

It is my first visit "States"-side, and I have no idea truly what to expect after a childhood watching *Chips*, *The Streets of San Francisco* and *The A Team.*

Those tv programmes, or "shows", had been about glamorous (or less glamorous) Americans on the West Coast—East Coast was Frank Sinatra, cops dressed in navy (I think of *Top Cat,* the cartoon) and Central Park.

In my International Relations class last semester, I noted what the Gold Standard was, but in another sense of the international, also noted we had an entire coterie of American girls all on exchange, from the US Midwest at a time I could only place New York, Los Angeles and Chicago on the map. Many of us dressed in shabby student rigs, but these wholesome college girls dressed as if they were VIPs at Brooks Brothers. One told me with not a hint of irony that things were "likely to be bigger and better".

We arrive on cheap Air India flights to see for ourselves the hustle and bustle of New York City streets, passing through Queens, streets full of graffiti—*Boyz N the Hood*—style. All we seemed to be missing was 1980s ghetto blasters, break-dancers and young men in baseball hats sitting around on house steps. We cross a bridge to get to Manhattan, heading to Harlem. Here we see archetypal yellow taxis, and find our accommodation in Columbia University's Halls of Residence off Broadway. Local shops have steel shutters over them, and enduring jetlag, the night is noisy with sirens and low-level noise.

After a walk around Central Park in the morning, with roller skaters zipping past, leaving not much of a margin—we are thrown into low-intensity training based on mini-lecturettes and group role plays. This is reinforced by question-and-answer sessions (none are to be of any real use), and a girl has a response for everything. The rest of us take notes and pin our ears back.

A coach busses us upstate towards the foothills of the Catskill mountains to Camp Bo Pa named after Red Indian native origin. It's a Jewish camp targeting wealthy New Yorkers organised on classic lines, with rows of cabins around a swimming pool, central dining area and hall, with a lake off to one side. The owners live in a swanky villa just off campus and drive around in a Lincoln town car.

\*\*\*

I discover I have been appointed a Bunk Leader, even though I am barely a fraction older than the other counsellors. Two of them report to me having *graduated* from campers, styled "Junior

Counsellors". They have been coming to camp for years, and I rely on them to explain the intricacies of camp life.

Under our supervision, twelve boys aged ten. They are dropped off at a school carpark by their parents and we take our charges into our care with a "Good luck" and a slap on the back from the more agreeable fathers. They have the entire summer off by the looks of it and can't get away fast enough.

The boys start off well-behaved, if cheeky, and they are in high spirits as they unpack. The more thoughtful parents have packed an entire store of clothes. A counsellor takes a top bunk, and a boy takes the bottom. The first day or so, they are excited to be away, and are up with the lark before some sort of routine sets in. We are always alert for any of our charges going missing or being left behind, injuring themselves, or sloping off somewhere unnoticed.

"You get used to counting to twelve," one counsellor says.

We parade our little platoon over to meals—breakfast, lunch and dinner—I insist with my counsellors they are served before we are. Breakfast is any cereal you like, and bagels (with a spread called Lux.) We relax a bit as we work out the safe kids and the ones to keep an eye out for. We take notice of the boy that is inclined to be the showman, the kid who is left out of things; the natural sportsmen. There are the leaders and the charmers.

Most curious is their advanced knowledge of sex—and boy, did they pass it on to us. Teenage girls take it in turns to sit across from me at breakfast and are geed up in front of their friends to gauge my reaction to the offer of a most intimate act. They seem more knowledgeable than I am. My boys try it on, and I allow myself a smile at the way they push boundaries.

"Steve's smiling," they crow gleefully to each other.

They are a good bunch in the main.

Master Nudellman has a bowl haircut and is a principal mischief-maker and good all round sort. His mates instantly christen him "Nudellwomen" which doesn't surprise me.

One is a natural leader who knows everything and brings his influence to bear amongst the boys and with us, too. One, whom

I name "Punchy", has a tendency to sort out conflict with his fists.

Another wears round, wire-framed glasses and over-sized sandals which makes him look like a dead cert for a *Charlie Brown* character as he slaps along the path from the bunk to the dining hall. I name him "Peanuts". A junior counsellor wears a perpetual look of coolness—and holds his mouth slightly open in an insouciant relaxed way, baseball cap peak bent just right.

"It has to have a dip," he coaches us Limeys.

We look at our new caps again and inspect them—they don't appear to pass muster.

***

The boys' huts are on one edge of the camp and the girls are a respectable distance apart in their corner. The two camps are kept at arm's length. Regardless, this meant there is opportunity for boys to raid the girls at night, (I suspect the counsellors or older boys had some say in this idea). A few nights we awake to hear the girls' screams as they are squirted with shaving foam. The approach is either silent and stealthy, or an all-out attack. Fair warning is the light flicking on by a boy opening the door and reaching out for the switch.

Camp is run like a Swiss railway according to a timetable—on offer is go-karts, baseball, a death slide ("zipline"), fishing and boating at the lake. I catch a fish first-go with nothing but a hook and a piece of bread. And the less said about baseball, the better. I have several swings and miss each time, and it doesn't take long for them to catch me out from second base.

The boys' parents visit unannounced. A convention is that a proud father, considering a job well done, strides over and shakes your hand.

"Thanks for taking care of my son," he says.

As he holds my hand in a clasp, a 100-dollar note is pressed into my palm—a tip for the summer.

We retire to the bunk on a warm day, and exhausted, we

fall asleep whilst our little platoon run amok unsupervised. The door closed against the New York heat opens, and fathers step in to say hello—one wakes us up from our slumber.

"How are you? I'm Steve, I'm the Bunk Leader," I say sleepily. *No harm done.*

## 29 CAMP LIFE

The only respite from the grind of camp life is our weekly day off. Most take advantage of a lift to the local mall in a large Chevy truck and lose themselves in a movie. New York has recently removed its 55 mile-per-hour highway restriction, and my driver tells me he can now blitz to the mall at more like 75 miles-per-hour, which that big V8 will do without breaking sweat. For many of us, it's the first time we have seen a shopping mall, or even know what one is.

In the 1970s, my mother and I visited the Pentagon in Kent which would have been pushing it for the UK, but this is next level. At the exchange rate of about one and a half dollars to the pound, it's clear to us all we've been ripped off back home. We marvel at the sticker prices and fill up with CD Discmans, Levi jeans and sports gear to take back with us. A bloke from Sussex is obsessed with baseball caps, which he stacks up above his bed space.

It's also the first time I have seen a multiplex cinema with so many screens. Only the Odeon, Leicester Square can compete. The summer blockbuster I am interested in is *First Knight*, and I pay for my ticket, excitement rising. Of the few people in there, did anyone even know there is a Hollywood star in their midst?

I watch each scene like a hawk ready for the one. With no inkling of when it might come, I am exhausted by half-way. It doesn't completely escape me the movie is perhaps a bit of a dud. Two women behind me are restless and whisper to each other. I don't care they were talking about Richard Gere.

"Girls–I'm in this movie, shut up!" I say eventually.

That seems to work.

Our fight scenes come right at the end of the story, and I'm pretty sure I spot myself on a balcony above Sean Connery. That's it—I'm immortalised on the silver screen. I've only got to wait for the release on video in the New Year to confirm it.

Relationships blossom between counsellors, and boy, do the boys notice. I often speak with an Australian girl from New South Wales, she's pretty and down to earth in an Antipodean way.

It is hot, but sometimes the heavens open and we are saturated in a downpour. This is a cue for the kids to find an opportune hill and set up a mudslide, but no one breaks a bone, nor gets hurt. The next day, we visit a theme park over the state line, and we head down the New Jersey Turnpike.

"What the hell is a *turnpike*?" asks Alex, one of the UK counsellors.

It's the main highway to New Jersey, south of New York. When we arrive at our park, we're expedited through the entrance. It's all going swimmingly, and we are steering our kids in small convoys, grinning from ear to ear and swapping tips about the rides and attractions.

"Steve, I get nauseous," "Peanuts" says from behind his glasses.

We don't pay much attention, but the 20-something ride operator does when he must attend to a fouled-seat ten minutes later when our young lad loses his mid-morning snack. We'll know for next time.

***

In time, of course, the boys rename camp to Camp No Shit Pit as the novelty wore off, and life took on more of a *MASH* feel. Our Group Leader installs a metal speaking-alarm clock above his head which rouses us from our sleep with a war cry each morning:

"Time to wake up! Time to wake up!"

"Shut the **** up," the boys would cry.

The boys, of course, sleep in, and in dirt-streaked clothes, allow us to shepherd them down for breakfast. There are also pastoral issues to contend with which the training had only just prepared us for. "Punchy" is becoming an issue. He can't get on with the other boys and he flings punches easily, fracturing the bunk's cohesion. The Group Leader offers his advice and concludes,

"You're the man on the ground, Steve. Your decision."

After referring to the camp director up the hill in his house, and phone calls to the boy's parents, I decide he is to be sent home. His mother arrives and packs his things with my help. She sobs a bit, and I feel sorry for her.

An English counsellor is fascinated by UFOs, and one night he comes rushing in to tell us of strange lights in the sky. We bundle outside and we can't see much; maybe it is for his own entertainment. Other night visitors are racoons and skunks who are a novelty to the Europeans. The only known antidote to a skunk's spray is tomato juice should you disturb one on the front porch, so we are told.

While everyone sleeps, for a few weeks I sit in the low tungsten light of the sick bay and write an essay on Employment Law to submit in lieu of the unit I had failed in my final semester. In with me—kids ravished by insect bites or feeling off-colour, or homesick. I am to bed late and early to rise, needing an extra cup of coffee at breakfast. I'm almost done with this regimen one morning when Alex says,

"There's another aerogramme for you, Steve," he announces, sounding a bit peeved.

He reckons I get way too much mail from home. Under a brace of aerograms is a white envelope with familiar handwriting. It's from Rachael, and a sixth sense tells me this is mail I can't miss. I can smell the hint of perfume on the notepaper after ripping the envelope open.

Closer inspection reveals it's a "Dear John" letter, a classic for the ages, too. I read it quickly once, then a second time slowly, and put it in my pocket. I sit on the bunk steps and look out to the swimming pool.

*Rachael is calling time on our relationship.*

It's all simply too much for Rachael.

She needs me around, and a major sign with a new client is taking her away from the south of England. It's a downer, but it's all my fault for being not being there, chasing *stuff*. I accept, though, I won't have any regrets with her decision. I must get through my commitments, and retake that exam.

I tell Alex at breakfast. A few of the girls are sympathetic when they find out, particularly the girl from New South Wales. I'm a bit down, but soon get back on track.

***

Camp concludes in August, and Alex and I join forces to see the north-eastern seaboard on a whistle-stop tour. We will use the US coach network Greyhound to get around between state capitals and plan an epic run to the Canadian border at Niagara Falls, and to Toronto, so we can say we have been to Canada.

First port of call is New York city for an official day out. We walk down 5$^{th}$ Avenue and ride the elevator to the top of both the World Trade Centre and Empire State Building. We catch the ferry to Staten Island and back, which lets us get close to the Statue of Liberty. We break our journey to Niagara by stopping in Buffalo, at the end of New York state, where we find a youth hostel with a good rate. Alex notices there is a baseball game on.

"Let's head over and take a look," he says.

Evening finds us sitting on the bleachers and fathoming out the game—we decide it's not quite like the UK game rounders.

In the morning, there is no time to waste as the coach to Niagara departs at 8 am. We had been tipped off to avoid the US side of the falls, so we cross the border, and disembark on the Canadian side. The other side is a drab collection of hotels. On this side, an impressive strip of shops and hotels, and we can stand at a viewpoint and look across to the famous Horseshoe to see tourists approach the cascades in a boat.

"'The Maid of the Mist'," reads Alex, looking at the sign for the attraction.

We press on to Toronto, taking advantage of the short-lived

Canadian summer. A sign of the times: Bill Gates' Microsoft is releasing *Windows 95* and they've plastered the entire CN Tower in bunting from top to bottom. Planes with banners fly overhead and there is a bit of an industry buzz.

Next, overnight to Boston, where we cruise the harbour and visit Civil war outposts, and a short excursion to Harvard to see the famous college.

Finally, in our whistle-stop tour, we hit Washington DC, where we visit the Air and Space Museum, and marvel at the size of the Lunar module. At the National Gallery, I buy the print by Thomas Eakins of a rowing pair. We walk the length of the mall past the pool to the Wall of Remembrance and Tomb of the Unknown Warrior. It's then time for me to return to London as I've got the pesky exam to retake.

## 30 A DAY IN COURT

With nothing left planned, it's time to consider the trip down to Africa to join my crew. The final countdown? For better, or for worse, Rachael is not going to be around. One hurdle is the exam I had to take, though, which I sit two days after I return from the US. I make my way a last time to campus and sit in a small room with a clutch of resitters in the same situation as me. I have crammed my text on the plane from New York and have drunk a lot of coffee, all the more to stay alert.

There's a studied fug of concentration as we write for a few hours, knowing this is the session that will make or break us. No one says at a word at the end, and we all slip away to wait for the result.

*I'll be ok.*

Whilst going over gear for my sailing trip, I receive a call from a member of the Scottish courts who wants to come down to question me about the fracas in Scotland months before. He is wanting to move things along quickly for a timely resolution.

"I'm planning on coming down to London next week. I'd like to interview you, get your story, and the facts, for court. Nothing for you to worry about personally," the lawyer says.

"I want to head off soon. I've only got a few weeks," I reply.

"Never mind, we plan to get you here in days," he clarifies.

He turns up at the flat, with a bulging tatty briefcase of the sort that visiting doctors used to use. It's expanded to the max, with an enormous file balanced in the opening. He's a bit unkept, even rather slobby, and is perspiring. I offer him a cup of tea and he spreads out papers on the table and we go through the incident, as best I can recollect. He's obviously got the statement the police took and is looking for inconsistencies the defence can seize on.

"Now then, Stephen," he says, eventually.

*Stephen. It's Steve, mate.*

"Call me Steve," I insist.

"Right. Steve will do," he replies.

"We've fixed the date for the appearance. You need to be there as our witness. It will just be you and a single defendant. You've nothing to be concerned about, this is not about you," he continues.

*Great.*

"Yup, I'll be there. No problem–I'm a student, I've got time on my hands," I answer confidently.

*It might be a fun day out. Maybe they'll cross-examine me.* I figure it's a chance to learn something.

"The court will pay your rail fare up there, you'll need to take the night train," he concludes.

*That same train.*

So, yet again, I'm on the overnight sleeper from King's Cross. I'm losing track of the number of times I am making this journey north of the border. I'm the star witness, in fact the only witness, in the case for *Malins vs a local Scotsman*. The Scottish Crown Prosecution service has got my full attention by the promise of an all-expenses paid trip, even if accommodation wasn't on offer.

On the train, I get talking to a bunch of people seated at my table. A soldier from a Guards battalion returning from leave tells us about his trip to Kenya. The girl opposite leads the conversation. By about 1 am, unprompted, she steers us around to her impressive art portfolio and we admire it with bleary eyes.

I am greeted by the lawyer standing in the cool lobby of the courthouse in Glasgow.

"Steve. You made it. Great–take a seat."

He informs me at the last minute, high noon, if you like, that the defendant has entered a Guilty plea and will accept sentencing. That's fine by me.

"Good, I'll go and get a tea," I reply.

They say that everyone gets their day in court—I get mine returning to the steps of a courthouse on a grey day in a provincial Scottish town on the other side of the UK.

"I'll come with you," the lawyer steps out with me.

"Forgot to say Steve, get to the office and they'll pay you cash in lieu of compensation for the injuries you received."

*Again, fine by me.*

The lawyer has nothing to do, so we adjourn to a café a few doors down. He gets a tepid coffee in a mug; I get breakfast tea. The lady behind the counter discharges hot water into a cup from a hot water service and the tea bag floats to the top of the cup like a boat on a King tide. She hands it to me, tag hanging over the rim. The lawyer gets a coffee and a cookie. We take a table next to the menu hanging on the wall, and riffle through the newspapers.

*Not much happened overnight.* He tells me about his wife and children out in the suburbs and reflects on how busy he thinks he will get the rest of the week. He doesn't mind his work. When it's time to go, we stand up and push our chairs in.

"Good luck," he calls. "Stay out of mischief."

The Intercity 225 races back to London, and I mull over the prep for my sailing trip next week. I'm organised and ready to go. Everything else is off the table, or on hold.

Back in London, I pick up the mail lying on the doormat. There's a white envelope with the university frank on the postmark addressed to me.

*This could be it.* This could be ominous. I rip it open with nervous fingers, and take out a single sheet of typed paper, again, folded in to three. It's my exam results. My heart is in my mouth as I count down the exams and find the single updated line I need. My eye finds it in a microsecond and burrows in on the text.

I've passed the last exam by the skin of my teeth. A pass is a pass. I'm going to be awarded a Lower Second class degree with

Honours.

*Not too shabby considering.*

# 31 PALM SUNDAY

*The art of the sailor is to leave nothing to chance.* Annie Van De Wiele

Winter is drawing closer. The leaves have finished falling off the trees in the avenues around our house and lie on the pavement, and the chill pinches the face when you venture down the road for a pint or a newspaper. I've invested in a pair of deck shoes and a waterproof, and packed for temperate and tropical climes. All I have to do is grab my backpack. Departure day is tomorrow.

I won't be travelling with so much ease, though. London Heathrow may not be that far, but as the airline Britannia operate their charters to the Canaries from Gatwick, I will have to set my alarm for two am, to catch the night bus to Central London to make the first train to the airport. Gatwick is not as big as its better-known brother, but plenty of flights leave to warm destinations from one of its two terminals.

I end up in the South terminal waiting for the boarding call to Las Palmas finding my rightful, if not habitual, place amongst the great "unwashed" in variations of shell suits and leisure wear.

Las Palmas, the capital of Gran Canaria, is the heart of an island which is nothing more than a volcanic outcrop, about 100 miles off the Moroccan coast. The sub-tropical waters and year-round-sunshine make the Canaries a tourist mecca for holidaying Brits.

It's only a five-hour flight, not much less than London to New York, and our great circle route will take us over the Atlantic as winter approaches home. We touch down at the airport sited on the eastern side of the isle. It handles several million passengers a year and is the fourth busiest in Spain—even the space shuttle can land there—and apparently, there's a "Top Secret" NASA tracking facility.

I find it's pleasantly mild on disembarking at 22 degrees Celsius, agreeable after a UK autumn. Apart from the Spanish signage, with armed policeman dressed in military-style uniforms, and blue skies, I could be in any exotic place. It doesn't take me long to get to the bus station and locate the departure bay I need, which saves me finding someone who understands English.

A local bus whisks me from the town to the marina. Not many people share it with me for this trip out of town; most of the locals would have arrived during the rush hour. The driver has a local radio station on, and an announcer can barely contain his excitement as he babbles—telling stories in a Spanish lisp, the soft sibilant S of the accent coming across the air.

The roads are also quiet: we see farm pickup trucks and the terrain is dry and browning already. I am reminded of the Cypriot landscape, olive trees, and stunted shrubbery. It's funny to think I am not so far from the teams of British tourists on Tenerife, but the ride is not long.

Muelle Deportivo is the marina on the island, opposite the commercial port. It's larger than Rhu in Scotland, which befits one whose job it is to host the start point of a major oceanic rally from Africa to the West Indies.

I find a complicated spiders-web of boardwalks and decking spreading from the entrance, with all manner of boats of different shapes and sizes tied up. I scratch my head. I have no idea where to find *Derelict* and my crew, so I try a portacabin facing the water, housing the ARC rally office.

"Excuse me, I'm looking for *Derelict*, please," I ask the lady behind the Formica table.

She sits in front of a keyboard and VDU and is chatting with a man in a tropical shirt and ARC baseball cap.

"I'm sorry, we don't keep records of those," she replies apologetically.

She points me in the direction of the harbour master's office, where I can find the answer to my question. He is standing outside another portacabin in short sleeves, and when I walk up, refers my question to a girl who has a map on the wall of the marina, with vessels marked.

"Mooring 23," she says, smiling.

I'm pleased her English is better than my Spanish.

I lug my gear over to the spot. There is a gap on the jetty where *Derelict* should be, which puzzles me, but the skipper of the boat alongside tells me she is in dry-dock.

I lean my pack on a bollard and rest my shoulders, looking out to sea, before making the last leg to the dock. Here, I find a concrete hard-standing and a hive of activity. Everyone here has a sense of industry. Boats are off the deck on racks or suspended from cranes or lifts. And it's here I finally locate my crew.

Knut is standing under *Derelict,* which is elevated on stilts like an Airfix model. He is short like me, with muscly calves, standing sturdily in canvas boat shoes. He wears a Rip Curl surf t-shirt. He has longish blond hair, with curls, staying true to his Teutonic origins. He's from Hamburg on the Westphalian coast, a likely seaport. The rest of the crew are sitting respectfully nearby, observing him, fetching things, or watching. For now, they are all talking in German, and it dawns on me my own school-boy German will not help me now. They introduce themselves:

Jurgen is a smiling and obviously funny man, with a twinkle in his eye; in his early sixties by the looks of it. I can't understand what he is saying, but I can tell he is going to be popular, and a vital crewmember. The others appear to defer to him as the natural second-in-command. As far as I can work out, he comes from a Bavarian German village in the south.

Wolf extends his hand next. He was educated in Stuttgart, tall and handsome, but quiet, with a full head of tidy black hair, running to shyness. He's recently finished medical school and is training to be a surgeon, but I can't fathom which specialty. I'll find it out later.

Rik is from Sweden, a few years older than me, with a hint of chubbiness around his midriff, and blond locks that sprawl, then contain in a ponytail to the rear. He holds a baseball cap in hand and appears genial—he has the advantage of speaking English as well as swapping into German, which will be a distinct benefit, given we are mostly a German crew. His main aim is to head off to Venezuela via the "ABC" islands of Aruba, Bonaire, and Curacao: our Atlantic crossing is the first stage in his own odyssey from Europe's north.

I'm in luck though—there is another native Englishman: Simon hails from the North of England and discovering I am from London has a quip about "softy southerners".

*We'll see about that. He has no idea.*

He's of medium height, wears thick glasses and has a slightly diffident disposition, often nudging his frames back up his nose and looking around as if he's working things out. He favours knee-length shorts and a polo top. He is a regular at a local sailing club on the north-east coast.

I shake hands with them all, and then turn my attention to the boat, the star of the show.

She is painted in a pearl white matt, with blue highlights, her pedigree—laid down in Hamburg, and registered to the same location. She is similar to my training ship, *Heavenly*, only longer in length and wider in the beam—at 42 feet bow to stern (all the better for rougher seas). Rather more up to date compared to *Heavenly* too, and I can only guess sized-up will ride the Atlantic swell better too. She is not the smallest boat in the fleet by any means, and I have no doubt she can get us across if we look after each other.

"Steve, you've joined at the right time. We are going to buy the food," Knut says in deliberate, accented English. "You want to come with us?" he adds. "Drop your gear off."

Rik places his foot against the foot of the ladder, and I climb up and negotiate the railing. I shrug out of my backpack straps and leave the pack behind the cockpit door. Looking around, I can see a fair way along the harbour and out to sea, where I can identify distant shipping on the horizon, and yachts inbound or outbound from Africa and Europe. Glancing below, I spot Knut scratching the nape of his neck and Jurgen lighting a cigarette. I go hand over hand, back down, facing inwards, and regain the safety of the hard standing.

With a nod from Knut, we walk out of the drydock as a group, Jurgen leading.

## 32 TAKING STOCK OF THE SITUATION

We stroll up to the marina entrance in a gaggle and jump on the courtesy bus to get to the supermarket in town, which deposits us near a service station. Ladies fill up diesel SEAT cars, and there's a dog and a cat lying on the ground in the corner avoiding the rainbow-coloured fuel spills. Now in town proper, we look around at the sights and sounds. Just being abroad seems to heighten the senses.

The supermarket is a larger store, with tins and produce on wooden pallets, all the easier for the staff to stock and replenish, like a German Lidl. It's busy with other crews milling about, all after the same provisions. We can see the sense of competition, and smell the fear of missing out. There is a scurry for the last remaining popular items, and disappointed grimaces from people who will have to go somewhere else.

Zigzagging up the aisles, we stock up on cans: tuna, beans, veggies, diced tomatoes, condensed milk; grapefruit chunks, and fruit salad; apples, bananas, oranges and pineapple. Everyone eyes up the snacks—family bags of potato crisps and chocolate bars; in new and unfamiliar packaging. Fruit is important—we are aware Vitamin C is still as relevant for us today, as it was centuries ago when someone realized Scurvy was a problem for sailors during the Age of Sail. In fact, it was in 1795, exactly 200 years ago, Gilbert Blane persuaded the Royal Navy to give lemon juice to sailors. I guess we can thank him for the expression "Limey".

Just in case we end up in the ocean awaiting rescue, a sober thought—we've also got a few days of emergency water in bottles, which we can easily throw into the life raft.

We must wait in an orderly line to pay: Jurgen stands in his baseball cap, a faded and softened t-shirt, wearing a broad smile and laps up the scene, making faces at us, and witticisms to his compatriots in German. He looks down a list and makes sure we have essentials, plus a bit more—and he also ensures he's got enough cigarettes to last him the trip. An attendant hands these over from a kiosk as boxes of ten in cellophane, and Jurgen takes them in to custody, looking pleased with himself.

"Danke," he says.

He's also quick to find a decorative display of whisky and spirits, and he turns and mimes drinking at us. The selection he picks will be for small restorative nips along our way. He'll oversee dispensing, I'm sure.

When we get to the end of the queue, the cashier tallies up the purchase on an old manual 1970s till which clangs and shoots out the cash drawer into his lap and displays a total, and we reach in to rear pockets for local cash to pay our share.

I scale the ladder and find my berth for'ard in the bow and get organised. I shake out my sleeping bag and wedge the backpack underneath. There are enough berths for all of us, no need to "hot bunk" or share, as if we're on a submarine.

We form a line and pass the groceries up under Jurgen's tutelage with Knut clarifying where things should go, like spare parts or emergency rations. The tins stack neatly, Tetris-like, wherever there is space, including under the floor. Crates of beer are put in a place where we know exactly where to locate them. Jurgen pins a new fire extinguisher to a bracket near the stove.

"Priorities," remarks Jurgen in an exaggerated accent. Safety *is* a priority.

"I'll take you over the gear, Steve," says Simon.

He shows me the type of things which could get you out of a pickle: bilge pump, fire blanket, spares, tools, and a power drill. You can go nuts in this category, but we've got the basics, plus a bit more. Man-overboard gear is important, too. We've even got a life raft, and an EPIRB, a beacon which we can set off to attract Search and Rescue. It goes without saying we each have a lifejacket and I make sure it's either on my bunk or within arm's distance. Wolf and I visit the marine shop and sort the batteries for the radios, taking them back to the boat under our arms.

I stop by for a chat with the Rally organisers back in the ARC portacabin where there is a flow of people dropping in asking for advice. Some are just friends passing the time of day. There is a small merchandise stall and changing my mind on a mug, I settle on a t-shirt with the Rally logo, and a list of all the boats on the back, noting our vessel in a sans serif font. I try on the t-shirt for size. The word *Derelict* sits on my shoulders.

The marina is busy as crews victual for the crossing. Some seem in danger of overloading their boats—we see a multitude of supplies tied down, even bicycles—useful for transport on the other side of the world. Calm heads prevail—or rather meet, and swap tactics on the jetty in a variety of languages, but English, is of course, the *lingua franca*. Knut gets into a breakfast discussion with Jurgen and Wolf about whether we can use two foresails to get us across, and not need a mainsail at all. If I am not mistaken, this means we won't need to gybe so much or worry about the boom coming over. That's my takeaway on strategy.

We head out for a briefing and a supper—a final meal before departure. Most of the people making the crossing attend, and the event supervisors have set up a small stage with mike and speakers for announcements. A local band has brought their amps. A young bloke hooks up an electric guitar and sings favourites in English with a Spanish accent. The crowd applaud after each one—as the evening progresses there's the odd catcall or whistle.

Supper is bar-b-que beef, or pork, or paella and rice with an accompaniment of mussels and various salads. As we are tucking in, a man approaches Knut—he crouches down level, so he can hear above the music.

There's an exchange in German.

Knut invites him to sit, and he draws up a plastic chair and they talk more. I think I can guess what is going on. It looks like he wants to cross the Atlantic and is looking for a crew he can join at this late hour. He has an opportunity he can ill-afford to miss whilst all crews are having dinner at this "Last Supper".

He must win Knut over first, as our leader, and Knut confers with the others, putting the question to them. I can't understand these exchanges and crane forward. As we are one team, eventually Knut speaks in English to me and Simon.

"This is Ulrich. He wants to come with us on the trip and I believe we have room, is that ok with you?"

I look at the faces of our crew, I don't mind if they don't.

"Sure," I say.

Simon has no issue with this and it's unanimous our ship's nominal roll has increased from six to seven. We're a full ship's complement.

Ulrich is lean, bearded, youthful and balding early—with a kind smile: he seems like a thoughtful soul. But he also might be an extra card we have in our back pocket, as he's a trained doctor, so it will be safer having him around. There are not enough berths, so he's going to have to share with Rik, but they'll organise watches so one of them can sleep. Ulrich organises his gear on board, and we make him feel welcome.

Properly fed and watered, we are now all set to go tomorrow. Let's hope we will have "fair winds and following seas."

## 33 MY, WE ARE ON POINT TODAY!

A brass band has struck up in the marina and is piping our departure like a Royal Navy port sending off a warship. Hundreds of spectators line the piers, jetties, and town shore, the best views taken early. There's a rock spit, a seawall, that extends out into the water of the harbour, and it's lined with families sitting on camp chairs and waving.

We've motored out into the harbour, excitement in our eyes, perhaps a bit of nervousness. We join the fleet who have congregated in the waters beyond the sea wall, where two boats are keeping station representing the start. For us, it's of course recreation, for other crews it's competition.

Before the start of races or rallies, all participant boats must cross the start after the gun, maybe in, as the nautical saying goes, in shipshape and nautical fashion. As they can't cross until the gun fires, boats in the fleet mill about as best they can, trying to time their next dash towards the line with the gun. Get it wrong, and you are sailing away from the fleet, or worse, you might collide with another boat.

Not all boats want to race and many circle further back, as spectators, waiting for a quieter start, allowing their betters and superiors a chance to vie it out at safe distance. Relaxed crewmembers perch on the side, legs dangling down—serious crews are at action stations.

*Creightons Naturally* and another large "maxi" yacht wage war for position with their professional and eager crews. *Derelict* is two-thirds of the way back, out of the melee, tacking around in circles, waiting.

Lunchtime comes and goes, and we are on deck with lifejackets on. Jurgen has a pleased and expectant look on his face. Simon is quiet and reflective, even a little bored. I'm watching carefully. Knut, as skipper, is at the wheel, in his element, Helly Hansen waterproof on, squinting into the distance, his curly locks waving in the breeze.

It's not that warm today, and we've all got a jacket on to ward off the chill. Simon remains silent and peers around at the boats, spray flecking his glasses. The German contingent talk amongst themselves, exchanging views and offering advice to Knut—he listens and has an answer for them occasionally.

BANG!

The sound of the cannon firing reaches us.

There's also a simultaneous radio call on the HF radio.

That's the signal to start, and although we are not in pole position or competing with the bigger boats to get off to an early lead, we cross the line in good order. We beat upwind in a respectable place about three-quarters of the way down the fleet. It's no surprise we are surrounded by boats. We pick a course that will avoid any collision. Crews not interested in racing choose different tracks heading off in different directions, as if they want to be free of the fleet as soon as possible.

We sail along the heading Knut has decided on, talking amongst ourselves, craning out to sea. Jurgen passes around sausage he has cut up with a sharp penknife he has on a lanyard secured to his belt, and offers up a bag of potato chips. We've acquired quite an appetite after all the excitement.

As the first day wanes, and darkens, I realise to my dismay I have a touch of seasickness and am excused strenuous duties for the time being. There is not much to do, in any case, apart from steer *Derelict* or take up slack on a sheet.

Once out in the Atlantic, we go into a routine that will be largely unchanged for days, if not weeks. Waiting and watching, navigating and steering, adjusting; winding down the clock.

\*\*\*

Early days see us making ground, banking the first of many miles to come. We get to know each other—our tastes, proclivities, and ambitions. We spot other boats on both beams. Some maintain station through the day: others making faster progress pull away over the horizon out of sight. We manage about three—four knots an hour, perfectly respectable. I log our daily distance in my notebook. We cover at least 100 nautical miles a day, in the best conditions, a bit more. You can either see it as not much or a lot: *Derelict* is continually making headway as long as we have wind. We don't pull over, or tie up to sleep—we are always on the move.

*World Cruising Routes* has established itself as a *de facto* bible for navigators. It's used to plan routes anywhere in the world, with thousands of landmarks that Knut can use as a waypoint. He uses these to work out a bearing we can follow using the chart.

I found a British Admiralty book *Ocean Passages for the World* dating from 1895. Knowledge has been passed down for many years. We will stand on the shoulders of giants.

The direct route across the earth point to point, a straight line, is a "great circle" due to the earth's curvature. I know airlines fly them across the globe to save fuel.

Saint Lucia is about 2,700 nautical miles from our start, but winds and weather will dictate the actual route. Some boats favour the direct line, but others head more south towards Cape Verde to pick up better trade winds. It's also a diversion for those who run into early difficulties and need repairs, or God forbid, medical attention. Knut prefers this popular run southerly along the African coast before turning out towards the Caribbean. There's an old saying: "head south until your butter melts".

I was under the impression that we would be rolling the ocean's wave, from white tip to white tip, crest to crest, up and down, hanging on, shouting to be heard above the incessant noise. In fact, it's altogether a calmer experience.

It was a bit of novelty to realise you don't see far in the ocean. I had expected to see further. Looking from *Derelict*, we appear to be on a modest table-top of water. The apparent horizon doesn't seem far, so our immediate world seems tiny, as if we are in a goldfish bowl, held by a giant, sort of a nautical *The Truman Show*.

Our world shrinks accordingly and becomes insular. The horizon, when visible, is straight as a die, but *Derelict's* hull is often slanted, and this takes getting used to. Sea-faring birds and wildlife are ever present, and fish ride our bow wave as we transit the waters of the Atlantic.

*It's really happening.*

Evenings are balmy, and a chance to recover from the heat of the afternoon. We come to enjoy this time. As the temperatures drop, the humidity falls out of the sky.

The light has a mesmerising quality in the evening, with the sun so low, and if it's filtering through cloud cover, it saturates our tanning faces and presents our sailing clothes in glorious technicolor. We bask in the healthy and beautiful glow. Rik's long hair hangs in curls; I'm pretty sure I look bedraggled and flecked in saltwater—there is no mirror. The Germans consult and talk amongst themselves in civilised and cultured tones, breaking into peals of laughter occasionally. Simon and I are at a disadvantage, having no fluency or any conversational aptitude. For all we know, they could be talking about us.

I get to know Ulrich. He's a good bloke. When he removes his t-shirt, he is pigeon-chested, even a bit emaciated looking. Possibly in gratitude we have taken him at short notice, he returns the favour by cooking the first week, and taking more than his fair share the second. I help him peel a bag of potatoes, and as the skin comes off, the bowl between us, we face each other, knees almost touching. Ulrich tells me about his medical training and life in Germany. He lives near the Mosel, as it streams down from France into Germany. He's not a sailor, by training or inclination at all, but we're glad to have his company, as you never know when we might need to call on his skills.

Jurgen drops a fishing line over the stern and stands on the rod to secure it, chattering away as always. We watch and listen.

With *Derelict*'s hull running through the water, he can trawl for fish. Rik wants to see how far he can cast, and he grabs another rod.

He opens the bail and whips the line into the sea, but it doesn't carry far, so he tries again, with Jurgen providing feedback. On his fourth attempt, the weight carries the hook a fair distance, the reel unwinding in a frenzied whir—we hear a satisfying plop as the sinker hits the water tens of metres from the stern.

"*Gut, gut!*" Jurgen says.

Rik flicks his wrist to close the bail, then winds the reel handle to take up the slack. Now he needs to wait for the bite. As we chat, our eyes flit to the rod tip for the characteristic twitch, then away to each other to continue the conversation.

"You're on!" cries Simon.

Rik's rod bends alarmingly. He grabs the rod and winds in carefully and slowly. In time the fish comes out of the water, wriggling, and Jurgen reaches out with a gloved hand to take it inboard where he drops it into a bucket on deck. He filets it skillfully, showing off somewhat. He removes the steaks in a knife pass along the spine, leaves the tail in the bucket for burley, and the head goes on a hook for bait whilst it is still fresh.

The ancients might have worked out how to fish with hook, or even tickle freshwater trout in streams, but we get similarly lucky when flying fish land on deck, instantly gasping for water, their gills twitching, poor things. They are tiny, and not much of a feed; but still good eating for those of us looking to try something new. Baked in the oven for an hour in foil, our catch is delicious with lemon and rosemary, which Jurgen has kept especially in a jar. We sit in the cockpit in our fleeces and shorts, and eat the filleted flesh with a beer, which we have rationed on board, like Royal Navy matelots.

When night comes, the air cools, and one by one we head down to our bunks, leaving the pair on watch to maintain *Derelict*'s heading using our compass. The old Polynesian voyagers would set a heading by a star near the horizon, switching to a new one once the first rose too high. Early

STEPHEN MICHAEL MALINS

# Celestial navigation.

## 34 IN THE DOLDRUMS

*There is nothing more enticing, disenchanting, and enslaving than the life at sea.* Joseph Conrad

Those first days, Knut wants to get as much out of the wind as he can, and fusses over sail. To start with, we had our gib up, a smaller foresail, but when the wind is favourable, he gets us to switch to the genoa, a larger sail that can take advantage of these better conditions. We return to the gib if the wind gets too strong. It's a bit of a faff.

Knut occasionally says something, and everyone goes to assist. I have given up trying to react first as most of these commands or requests are in German, so take note of what is close by, like a winch or a sheet I might need to be on the end of. I'm perfectly happy to be ship's boy.

*A little knowledge is a dangerous thing.*

Owing to my native English-speaking ability, I've been assigned the duty of the daily check in, and by default the radio operator, which sounds important.

I have to pass on our location every day which I read from the GPS. In the old days, sailors relied on knowing what the time was, and took a reading with their sextant at local noon, and used an almanac to find their Longitude and Latitude.

It's also a way of passing the time and gives me plenty of opportunity to inspect the chart and our progress between Africa and the islands of the Caribbean chain. The chart shows the coasts, and the shallows and the deeps of the North Atlantic waters. Numbers like *3444* call out depths, in metres, presumably. There's no chance we will run aground though, and there are contour lines showing common depths, like on an Ordnance Survey land map.

I can see islands that I had never heard of, for example, the *Arquipelago Dos Acores*, which on closer examination turn out to be the Azores. These are the feature called out on the weather forecasts on the radio back home. Our destination is on a line of longitude 60 degrees (west) and about 15 degrees (south) placing it square in the tropics, which seems reminiscent of old stories of people drinking tonic water laced with quinine to ward off malaria. It conjures up images of men in crisp white shirts and shorts, with knee-height socks on balconies enjoying a sundowner.

If we were physically crossing the Equator, we'd "cross the line".

Tradition dictates that all sailors who cross have to go through the trials. We'd have to take part in the time-honoured ceremony which involves dressing up, (or undressing) and performing bizarre rituals. We will escape these, and our dignity will remain intact.

My daily ritual, the radio call with ARC Control, starts at 12 noon. It will soon be obvious if a mishap befalls a boat out here on the high seas. The organisers can't help directly, but can respond nearby boats to assist, or presumably vector in Search and Rescue ships into the area. I also keep a tiny little diary on hand, to record any salacious situation I hear about.

Men and women from the fleet, vessel by vessel, stand by on channel, in alphabetical order, to await Jimmy, our leader's call: as he has to work through quite a list, he proceeds as fast as he can. Today, he works down to near us on the order:

"And, *Bravo.* No 124! Your position *please*," he says, sounding jocular.

(We still have some way to go.)

I'm soon in line, ten boats next, restless, as my time approaches.

Five boats closer—I shift likewise nearer to the edge of my seat, as if that will help my broadcast reach further across the waters between us.

"*Derelict!* Your position, please," he asks again.

*Here we go.*

I compose my thoughts and depress the switch on the mike, which stops all static.

"Hello ARC Control, this is yacht *Derelict*–our position is figures: 1133 1313. Over."

*That's it.*

I release the button and the sound of static comes back to all listeners. My diction was slow, my pace deliberate, and Jimmy on "control" acknowledges my call immediately.

"Well *done, Derelict*! Received," he says in sudden high spirits.

Looks like I've passed the test, and well, too. They taught us well in the military.

Other boats in the fleet, out of range of control can relay via closer boats using them as a "middle-man". ARC Control has trouble hearing an update from *Deuteronomy*.

"Hi *Deuteronomy*–nothing heard, can anyone relay?"

We hear silence for a while, and then I interject.

"Hi ARC Control, ah, we had comms with *Deuteronomy,* and I have their position–over."

"Thanks, *Derelict, Send,*" he says.

"ARC Control, *Deuteronomy* position is: 1212 1121. Over."

He reads it back to me and I confirm.

"Out to you."

I sign off.

*None of this "over and out" rubbish they use in the movies.*

All is well.

We can perch in the cockpit all hours of the day, but we're not all required to be there, and it's a stretch to fit us all. Sometimes, we doze on our bunks, or crouch upfront on top, attached by a safety line, or lie on the fibreglass, towel covering the face. At least two of us are officially on watch, one at the wheel steering a heading. Some boats use wind-vane steering systems to keep on course, but we want one person on watch all the time—and they might as well steer.

Some skippers run shifts in such a way that each crewmember can take a night off. As a group of seven, we will work in pairs on "watches", with Ulrich augmenting a pair.

There's a milestone of sorts when we cross into the Tropics on Day Three, crossing the Tropic of Cancer, 23 degrees north of the Equator. We've sped up a bit. The weather stays warm, it's more of the same: long days of sunshine, and it's rare there is much cloud at all. And in fact, we avoid any rain, staying dry, the weather clement. As we approach the Equator, the days lengthen, and they are almost as long as the breezy nights we experience, although we won't, of course, cross the line.

We swim to alleviate the oppressive warmth on some days, and the fact we have no shower.

Wolf emerges up top in a daring pair of European bathers, Speedos, and a set grin on his face, and one leg at a time, swivels over the rail and drops into the swell, ducking his head under the waves. He smooths his hair from his eyes and beams broadly at us, pleased with himself. We keep a weather eye on him, as we don't want to lose a man overboard. Rik follows his lead and jumps in next, in a pair of surf shorts—a little tyre of fat around his belly, and shakes his head to flick the salt-water out of his eyes.

We wonder if there are sharks about—Oceanic Tipped sharks come to mind—the ones renowned for taking survivors from shipwrecks, as recounted by sailors in the Pacific in World War Two. I'm pretty sure there won't be any Great Whites or "white pointers" near here though—they inhabit the coastlines of the US, South Africa and Australia in cooler waters.

"I'll let you know if I see one, Rik," I tell him, giving him the thumbs up.

It's an exhilarating and sobering moment when we recall there is nothing below our feet but the floor of the Atlantic Ocean. Here in the ocean, the average depth is three-and-a half kilometres. For all we know, though, we're atop a trench, which means it's even further down. There are three in the Atlantic alone. The Puerto Rico Trench at 8,648 metres is not so far from our destination.

It's more likely, though, if anything, we are above the Mid-Atlantic ridge, a sort of mountain running along the ocean floor. But whichever way you look at it, we're in *deep water*.

## 35 WILD SARGASSO SEA

"**S**teve!–It's your watch, wake up."

I wake from a dream to hear the following sea behind us, but also the bow of *Derelict* cutting through the water near my ear: it's as if I am in a hammock suspended from palm trees. But I'm not, it's just my turn on watch, which I take with Wolf—that's almost every other night. Knut has worked his roster so that working in pairs, we only have a handful of watches on the trip.

These night watches are a good time to be about. I'm up quickly and unselfishly, craning to hear if there is any update or information I need.

I climb up the ladder on to deck, and nod at Knut, who I am relieving. He shows me the compass bearing. Wolf joins us, and I show him—he also nods to confirm. Knut coughs, yawns, and prepares to go below to sleep.

There's a smidge of light up top from an exterior light, running lights on the mast, and the faint glow from the interior which is the chart table light. I stir as my senses dial in to the night: vision, hearing, smell, then touch, as I grasp the cool metal of the wheel. Even the taste of the sea.

I hear nothing but the air streaming through the rigging, and the squeak of a sail, or the screech of metal ring on fibreglass. Some boats come with an auto-helm which keeps them running true, but we favour fronting up, taking turns. It gives us something to do.

It is delightfully mild, and I've only got an extra layer on over my sleep t-shirt, lifejacket on over the top. I step carefully over to the wheel, feet planted shoulder-width apart, hands at a wide "ten to two" and look up into the night sky. I can feel the progress we make as the hull rips through the ocean.

Wolf stands next to me but says nothing. I check my bearing and that we are still pointing in the right direction—heading for our next waypoint tens of nautical miles in the distance.

There is a shaft of moonlight across the masts, so it's possible to steer by the light of the full moon, as told in *The Owl and the Pussycat who went to Sea*. I note it is silver in colour, but the children's story is silent on this. There's a knack to being at the helm. I can't keep an exact course on the bearing. As *Derelict* deviates from the heading, I bring her back, each pull of the wheel asking the rudder to brake *Derelict*'s drift through the Atlantic waters.

And as a member of the ship's company, I get the sense of being completely isolated. There are six crew all within a dozen arms' lengths—but most of humanity is thousands of miles away to the west in the US and to the east in Africa, and I've got no way of knowing, precisely, where any other yacht is.

We could sink in a trace, and no one would ever find us or work out what happened, only that we didn't show up on the next radio check-in. I wonder if my parents are worrying, what my brother is doing right now. I stare up into the rigging, up as well as around, and I get dizzy—until I have to come back and glance at the compass.

It's a wonder to see the constellations, the Milky Way, the moon, and dozens of shooting stars for hours. Below my feet, there are many thousands of metres of depth with strange and unknown creatures.

*Nothing* around me, that I can detect—yet our tiny yacht is making headway in a huge ocean. It's a unique and privileged feeling to have, simultaneously, a huge, and, tiny space to yourself.

After my watch, I lie awake, my feet out of my sleeping bag allowing a draft to circulate.

I consider other sailing undertakings that have been a fair bit more strenuous than ours so far. I read a book about New Zealander David Lewis's solo crossing, and circumnavigation of the world at the 50th line of latitude in the 1970s, on board his small yacht *Icebird*. He sailed into the impetuous

Southern Ocean, probably the roughest in the world and then to Antarctica, which he then attempted to sail around. He didn't make it, and had to be rescued and spent the winter in Australia. He finally got to South Africa. Later, he also circumnavigated the oceans with his young family. It takes a special sort of bloke—and family—to do that.

***

Today, we sight yet more schools of flying fish—they often land in the cockpit and Jurgen will fry them up for dinner with a bit of butter from the ice box, a grin on his face, regardless of if he's on kitchen duty or not.

We are progressing to our next waypoint, but I've read about a section of the ocean called the Sargasso Sea—there was a movie named after it a few years back, but it's not the stuff of fiction. It's a calm sea, known for brown seaweed, but blue water. In July 1969, British businessman and amateur sailor Donald Crowhurst disappeared there with his yacht. Bermuda, which sits on its own in the Atlantic miles from the other Caribbean islands, is on the western fringes of the sea.

*Did the Bermuda Triangle get him?*

Simon schools me in currents and the water. I find myself fascinated by ocean winds and currents which dictated the route the old merchants could sail. It turns out that the Portuguese couldn't hug Africa to return to Europe from the Americas. They had to sail out of their way north of the Azores. On the routes to India, ships would swing out to Brazil before turning back along the edge of Africa and then around the Cape.

At the Equator, further south, there is an area known as the Intertropical Convergence Zone, where the north-east and the south-east trade winds converge. Cloud forms there, and the rainfall creates the wet and dry seasons of the tropics.

# 36 SOUTHERN OCEAN

I man the radio at noon, discharging my duty, slumped over the table and my notebook. The daily calls are getting mundane, nothing's reported, and there's not even idle chit-chat. One day, though, after the call, there is a bit of excitement.

"ARC Control, this is yacht *Turino,* message, over."

I hear this right after the daily whip-round when traffic falls off, so my ears prick up. There is no immediate response from our illustrious leaders. Again:

"ARC Control, this is *Turino*, message, over."

This is followed by another call, but still no answer.

*They can't hear them.*

I figure they might be out of range—but maybe I am in a better position to relay.

"*Turino*, this is *Derelict*. I can relay over?"

I hear a worried, even agitated, female voice on the net. She pauses, then says,

"Er, this is *Turino*, we have a medical emergency, suspected broken leg, over."

Wolf has been listening in to proceedings, as he wants to improve his English. He's now also leaning forward, and I glance at him.

"Okay, *Turino*. This is *Derelict*, want me to inform control? We'll get you some help–wait out," I ask.

My heart starts beating faster and I crane forward, headphones pressed to my ear. I need to be as efficient as possible, and not muddle or confuse things. I depress the toggle on the mike.

"ARC Control, this is *Derelict*. Relay please," I ask.

I don't need the phrasing to be perfect, as long as they get the intent. Now ARC Control comes in, although fading somewhat.

"ARC Control, hello, go ahead, *Derelict*."

"ARC Control, *Derelict*. Relay from *Turino*. I say again TURINO.

We have a medical situation on *TURINO*, [I emphasise the name] her signal strength is weak. We have a surgeon on board *Derelict* and will provide assistance," I say, ensuring I speak clearly, with pauses.

I don't want to step in, unnecessarily, here, but control comes back to me instantly.

"Thanks *Derelict*, for relaying, please stand by and keep us updated. Go to channel 14. Over."

"Roger, ARC Control, out to you," I finish for now.

*Looks like we dealt with the scenario as best we can.*

Simon has turned up and listens in without saying much. I tell him what has happened.

We get an appraisal of the situation. Through static and relays from other boats, it turns out that a woman on board a fleet vessel has injured herself in a fall, and it appears like it's a broken right tibia.

Wolf and I switch places, he in front of the chart table and me taking notes. Ulrich is asleep on his bunk, and we decide we can let him rest for now, one medic is enough.

Our patient is in a lot of pain. She needs stabilising, so Wolf, using as much precise English as he can muster, talks her crew through splinting the leg. He speaks economically, finding each word he needs—and we crane forward listening in. Small miracles: the break is not complicated, as they say in medical circles—no ugly, open wounds or blood loss. A severance of a vein or artery could be fatal, but this one looks like a clean break. A major trauma, if not critical, right now.

Wolf talks them through dressing and suggests pain relief. The best painkiller they have is Panadol and this woman is going to need lots. And when ARC Control comes back into range, they recommend the crew that they divert back to Cape Verde immediately. They come back on the net a short while later with an affirmative:

"Okay, we are proceeding back to Cape Verde."

Later in the cockpit, Simon tells me about the sort of sailing accidents he's heard about. A common injury is the boom coming over, as I've heard, and knocking people unconscious or even off boats. But there's also burns from the galley, fishhooks in fingers, arms, even heads, and big bangs and bruises, trauma —or breaks—from falling over, like our young victim.

He hangs around and is quieter for a while. I sense something is wrong and look up, smiling. He moves forward to get the new carton of wine we've opened and comes back and sits nearby.

"Want a drink, Steve?"

Simon pours a glass of red wine into a tumbler from a carton of wine. He's quiet still, but I sense he has something to share. He confides in me he is not that well.

"Steve, I've got cancer. I've got about two years."

It's not an aggressive cancer, but it will get him eventually, he tells me. I'm appalled to hear this—you'd never guess.

"I'm really sorry to hear that, Simon."

*What the hell do I say to that?*

"Steve, my days are numbered, but I have accepted it, and this is my chance to have some time to see the world." It's as if he's practised saying it.

Later, it forces me to review my own reasons for taking this trip. I'm seizing every opportunity that comes my way relying on my sense of adventure, expanding my horizons. I'm learning about myself in the process. But setbacks and tragedy strikes us all—my aunt died last year of bowel cancer leaving my two cousins without a mother.

# 37 ON TOP OF THE WORLD

One night on watch, Wolf and I spot a vessel off our starboard bow. It's carrying lights for visibility. We can't tell which direction it's heading in at first.

*Is it going to hit us?*

Wolf leans forward to see. The moonlight grants him an advantage.

It's a ship with some sort of cargo. We have no idea what, nor can we spot a name. We turn on the VHF radio in case we need to get in contact. Peering into the night, we work out it's going to pass us safely with plenty of space to spare. No need to wake Knut or grab a signalling torch.

That's the sole night sighting we have after days at sea. It's one of two vessels we sight the entire trip. My mother had a book written by a woman, Rosie Swale, who after sailing around the world with her husband and baby, later sailed on her own across the Atlantic, and became becalmed in the Caribbean. She tells of the time she was almost run down by a cargo tanker.

\*\*\*

After lunch on Day Nine, Wolf goes forward to adjust the sail. He seems to be having difficulties. It doesn't budge; the sheet is taut and won't yield. He looks back at us.

It's jammed.

The sheet is hard up against the halyard line at the top of the mast—it seems like an insurmountable distance up.

Wolf scratches his head and calls out to his compatriots. Knut ducks out of the cabin where he's been making scrambled eggs in the galley. There's an intense debate in German, and Knut looks up, shielding his eyes from the sun. Jurgen and Rik join in, and Simon and I exchange glances.

I look at Knut expectedly. Spotting my quizzical gaze, he acknowledges us and switches to English and says,

"I'm climbing the mast. Looks like the line is stuck."

We nod. He needs to take care. He will use a safety rope, which we can take around the mainsail halyards, which are securely fixed to the mast.

Knut says something to Rik, and he rummages in a locker and retrieves a harness called a bosun's chair. Knut straps in and gets comfortable. Beads of sweat appear on his forehead, and he waves away Jurgen and Wolf, who have been offering advice.

He inches up, hand over hand, muscles bulging. Every few feet, Jurgen—a safe of pair of hands if ever I've seen them—pulls down on the safety line to take up the slack, should Knut fall, or the main line break. Knut is sweating with the effort, and I can see he's trying not to look down.

After an effort, he gets to within an arm's reach of the top, and looks down for the first time, allowing himself a grin in our direction.

"Achtung!" shouts Jurgen.

(*Danger*, I translate mentally, remembering my childhood *Commando* comic books.)

There's a bit of fumbling as Knut works quickly, but steadily, to work the jam free. The sea state is calm, he's thankful that there is no high wind right now.

"It's OK, yeah?" yells Simon.

Looks like he has done the trick—but he's not coming down until he's sure the job is complete.

"You don't want to go back up there again, mate," mutters Simon to me.

Knut starts on his way down, but not before he reaches carefully into his harness and frees the camera he's stuffed in there. With his feet wedged against the mast, he can use one hand to take a photo out to sea. He gets another of our sea of faces craning up. He's straining with all his fatigued arms nots to slip, and Jurgen once more takes his skipper's weight.

"*Nicht schnell! Nicht Schell!*" he warns.

"What's the view like up there, Knut?" I ask.

"*Est ist besonders gut,*" he replies. Really good.

*This* far in, I thought we would be riding the crests of an angry sea, whipped by rain and wind. I had convinced myself we would be hanging on for dear life to shrouds, rails, and taking up the slack on winches, craning to be heard above the noise. I know enough about racing, let alone cruising to work out that races are won and lost on route selection, wind, or sheer luck. Bad luck can happen to boats at any time, necessitating repairs.

For us, it's generally calm, and we lie in the cockpit for hours at a time, having to get up and stretch inactive legs by inching carefully forward to the bow and back again, holding on like Spiderman, both feet and a hand.

Our speed through the water is three to six knots, and at noon, I am still recording the distance. That seems like a crawl, but as long as there is wind, *Derelict* won't ever stop. Most days we make at least 100 nautical miles over the 24 hours—and one day, with better conditions and our genoa, we manage 120.

*I'm bored. Should I be? I'm on the trip of a lifetime.*

Today's a quieter day. We've read every single book on board in German, French or English, apart from myself and Simon, who can only manage our native tongue and we've exhausted that library too.

We have a few English-language books lying around in addition to the book of poetry I am dipping in to. I'm reading *Fatherland*—about what a German occupation of the UK would be like had they won the war. My earnest crewmates don't seem too bothered about this, not that I would cause an English-German scene.

## 38 A SPOT OF BOTHER

We sunbathe on deck topping up our tans. A bottle of sun lotion—factor eight—has the call, and does the rounds, and we rub it into each others' backs with a grunt of gratitude. As the end of our second week approaches, we are browning as nicely as a Thanksgiving turkey. One thing —no one thought to install a shade above the cockpit, say a "Bimini"-style awning, so that we can seek shelter. Wolf, ever the engineering genius, comes up with the idea of rigging up a tarp, and he spends an age tweaking it, so we get the welcome respite we need.

Our Germans think nothing of stripping off and sunbathing nude. Simon and I raise an eyebrow. I read once that nudism was commonplace in East Germany. It was a chance for people to enjoy a sense of freedom living under the rules of the same-same days of communism. Jurgen smokes the occasional cigarette— he is rationing his supply, pacing himself. He is careful not to burn himself and flicks his ash overboard.

"I want to give up," he laments.

*Sure.*

By Day 11, we hit the North Equatorial current in line with Brazil, one of the swirls of water that pass through these waters. There's no land mass to see on the chart, nothing at all. The closest land is the islands of the Caribbean. Cape Verde is well behind our stern to the east, too far to be a place to make for. The current might explain the distances *Derelict* is now covering. At one point, we make an impressive 200 nautical miles in a day. This is the most we've made so far, and we've made similar mileages in recent days.

Some of the practices we tried in Scotland do not apply here. We don't reef the sail at all, as the wind is constant. Knut switches to the spinnaker, which fills out before us with the wind behind us. We need to keep an eye on it—so we have three people on watch at night. If the wind picks up, we want to be able to kill it fast.

*Now* we are running before the wind.

***

Simon is sitting next to me on the backseat, in his rubberized foul-weather jacket, the afternoon is cooling. It's Day 15, our third week.

Looking at the chart, we are still miles from anywhere, but Brazil now seems a tantalising option. With Suriname to the south, Latin America seems not so far now. The Caribbean chain is now approaching to the west. Barbados is the closest isle now. It sits on its own, like a lone sentry for the island chain.

Simon is gazing up into the sky behind us. He's worried about its appearance. Not so long ago, it was calm, and we had blue skies. After lunch, we saw wispy streaks, which told him something.

"Look at those clouds Steve," he says.

"Why's that Simon?" I reply.

"Those clouds up there, that means–I'm pretty sure–a front is coming in, it's the leading edge. It's deceptive, right? They look nice, though, don't they?"

"They do mate," I concede.

A front can bring bad weather, a squall—high wind and heavy rain. The wind is the key concern, as we need to manage our sails and our passage through the waters.

Later, the pressure indicated on the barometer drops, and the sky takes on a moody appearance as higher clouds move in from behind, to the east.

Simon is still sitting in the cockpit. He hasn't moved: he looks at his watch.

"What do you reckon?" I ask.

"I'm a bit worried, Steve," he says.

If he's nervous, then I have reason to be.

"Looks like we've got a storm coming."

Knut and Jurgen agree we'll see wind gusts exceed the forecast, and that's high enough. Simon's an experienced sailor and the fact he is troubled makes me reconsider the situation. A storm that arrives and increases in force can knock out our sails, or we can broach, or roll, if *Derelict* is side-on to large waves.

Within a few minutes, the wind picks up and whips through the rigging, and it doesn't look like this is temporary. The others stand close and put on an extra layer to take off the chill. If nothing else, it gives them something to do. Jurgen glances at Knut. He can only tell us:

"We wait and see, *Ja*?"

*The calm before the storm, quite literally.*

If you've ever seen the George Clooney film *The Perfect Storm*, or read the book, even, about the marlin fishing boat that goes down with all hands, off Newfoundland in North American fishing waters, you'll know there's lots of detail about the way boats can flounder in high seas, even big ones with professional crews. There are fascinating pages and discourse of how boats ride gigantic waves and how helmsmen can steer them through. Boats are buoyant, of course, but dangerous waves can swamp a boat from above. It's a real danger in rough seas (or oceans). I don't believe we are at risk of a perfect storm, but we need to be mindful and ready.

The rain comes in suddenly from the north-east, increasing over time. The wind increases, perhaps to Force Seven strength, not quite a gale. The clouds thicken, and it darkens considerably. We are all wearing our waterproofs for the first time, and lifejackets are now a permanent fixture. We've been a bit slack recently.

A few of us are bunched up in the cockpit, but now anyone else out on the gunwale squeezes in, or heads down. Ulrich crouches on the ladder down to the cabin, looking alert.

So far, the situation is ok—we can deal with this sea-state and wind with good seamanship. We adjust the sails, reducing them so that we bleed off speed, and don't have unnecessary canvas exposed. We wonder if we can come down from that heightened sense of anticipation, waiting for the front to pass.

*We're coping.*

But it becomes obvious we will need to sit this out for longer yet.

The wind increases, but this is accompanied by worrying gusts—sudden blasts. These are the ones we need to watch out for. We have to hold on.

*So far, so good.*

Jurgen passes around a slab of Fruit and Nut.

"Chocolate, Steve?" he asks. It goes someway to dispelling the uncertainty.

*Derelict* rolls and yaws in the seas. We have been so spoilt up to now, this is alarming, and our senses are still heightened. Knut checks that anyone in the cockpit is tied on, has life jackets; changes his mind, and sends us below apart from Jurgen. We sit in the door craning up looking at his face trying to get a read. He braces his knees up against the wheel mounting and spins it back and forth in between waves aiming to be ready to climb the next one. I open a bottle of water and a packet of cream crackers.

"You need a rest, Knut?" asks Simon.

Knut declines for now. I reckon Jurgen will be up next.

This goes on for a while, and eventually Jurgen changes place with Skipper, giving him a break. Knut comes clattering down the ladder into the cabin, running a hand through his damp hair, reaching for a dishcloth. He had forgotten to put on his baseball cap.

Jurgen squints into the rain and out towards oncoming waves, and dutifully winds the wheel between wave crests and glances down at us once in a while. For once, he's not grinning.

After what seems like an age, the wind backs off. The sea calms down. It looks like we've come through this test.

It's then that Wolf, taking over the steering, realises we have a problem with our rudder—it's vague and unresponsive.

"*Achtung!*" he calls out to Jurgen, and they confer.

I eye him warily.

He's noticed we can't steer accurately. We're not sure how, but the sea state and constant spinning of the wheel have caused some sort of mechanical issue. We don't have the means for repairs—there is no help nearby, no immediate workaround, no *MacGyver* trick. So, we've lost the means of steering *Derelict* by ordinary means. This is a dangerous loss, as we can't align her in between crests of waves in any more rough seas we encounter.

There is, however, an improvisation—and Simon spots what they are up to.

"We can forget the spinnaker sail, and use the spinnaker pole over the back as a makeshift rudder, mate," he explains.

Simon takes the wheel, and Knut and Jurgen prepare the pole so that they can rig it out the back, taking line around the pole and stanchions on the stern to secure it.

Simon gives Knut the thumbs up.

It holds in place and works, to our satisfaction. This jury-rig will have to do until we make landfall still several days away. Saint Lucia is still 200 miles off, and Barbados, 100 miles away, is the closest island to bolt to, should we need to, even if it takes us off course. Knut decides to maintain three crew on watch tonight, just in case.

We will now limp to our destination.

By the morning, the sea state is still calm. The sun climbs up the northern sky from the east. In any case, it looks like the weather is settling for the next week with high pressure systems coming in. This is a welcome turn of events. We've not got that far to go now. The crew is in high spirits, a little tired, and perhaps a bit jaded with the relentless, repeating days that have passed. We are looking forward to landfall, a decent meal, drink, and the promise of warm, even still, Caribbean nights.

Although we can wash by going overboard, it's not the fresh water that we'd prefer. I'm feeling ripe, so I grab a bucket of seawater and wash my hair, dipping my head in.

Jurgen, ever the leader, and with his crew's welfare in mind, ducks down to raid a plastic box and nips back with cured ham, salami, and cheese. The entire ship's company cram together in the cockpit, knee to knee, all bonded as one and feast on the fresh food.

Will the Caribbean be all we've seen and heard?

## 39 DECLARATION OF INTENT

I n the same way the fleet dispersed as it left the Canaries and chose different routes across the Atlantic, as we near Saint Lucia, it makes sense that the vessels of the fleet converge as they near a common destination.

This is obvious when we sight our first fleet boat off the beam one morning on Day 16. We look through binoculars, looking for its name, trying to keep the glass still on the railing. As we draw closer, the font on the bow becomes readable. It's *Imp*. I don't recall seeing it in dock, or on the list at the ARC office, nor is it on my t-shirt. It looms larger, but maintains station off the port side on its own course. It's as if after several weeks in splendid isolation, everyone is a bit shy now and is hesitant to close up.

The next morning, Day 17, we see another boat on the port side, a dual-hulled catamaran.

The birds that we often see soaring over us become more frequent and, to my ears, vocal. It's even more exciting when we finally sight land on the horizon, and Jurgen is particularly delighted, a broad grin spreading from ear to ear, shouting, then gesturing at us to come and look. The Germans talk excitedly, and I go forward with Simon for photo opportunities. I've got both a compact camera and a SLR with slide film, cradling the two, SLR strap around my neck.

I hook my arm through the railing and take a few photos, also switching to 35mm slide, choosing 'Auto exposure' to get the shot.

We will approach Saint Lucia from the north-east, and skirt around to the north-west to find our port. The ancients used cloud to observe whether they are close to land masses or shallow sea and I look up hopefully, but see nothing, not a single reflection.

"When do you reckon we'll reach Rodney Bay, Simon?" I ask at last.

"Another night at this rate, Steve," he guesses.

\*\*\*

Up in the sunshine, leaning against the gunwale, I read up on the Caribbean, thumbing through my *Rough Guide* book. The large islands of Cuba, Jamaica and the Dominican Republic make up the Greater Antilles. The Lesser Antilles that runs north to south towards Brazil, is a volcanic chain of much smaller islands, which can be split into two groupings.

"There's the Leeward Islands, Steve, pronounced 'Looward' in the chain's north," Simon tells me.

The Windward Islands are the ones that lay further south— Saint Lucia is in the Windward islands. It's not obvious, but the west side of the island is in the Caribbean Sea: the east side faces the Atlantic. The country is only 280 square miles with a population of 180,000.

Simon and I get chatting about what the Caribbean means to us. I think of sundowners, Bacardi, and coke. Simon lists exotic James Bond locations, the international jet-set, coconut palms, and pina colada. I think of centuries-old engagements of the Royal Navy, pirates and treasure. I recall that Lord Nelson even hid his fleet in Saint Lucia from the ships of the French Navy barely two hundred years ago. We talk to late under the light of a waning gibbous moon, and then retire below.

As the sun comes up, *Derelict* is hugging the Saint Lucian coastline following it around to the harbour town, Gros Inlet. We're heading to the marina in Rodney Bay.

We turn a corner, and find ourselves in the Caribbean Sea at last.

We pass through a narrow channel to get to the sheltered bay. Fishermen handle nets and rods on the banks and look up as we cruise past. It's my first chance to peer at locals going about their every day. Some men chasing catch stand bare-chested in long dinghies, almost like pared-down gondoliers, only the fishermen are wearing smaller hats. They don't seem to be working too hard on a Caribbean roster.

Signal Peak rises at one side of the bay, ideal for an ancient watchtower, but the island has long been at peace.

The marina comes into sight. We see a dinghy with ARC blue and yellow bunting plastered all over it, and a smiling volunteer standing in the rocking bottom greets us. He gestures to a berth on one of several jetties that spiral out from the shore. The jetties closer to us host larger, and correspondingly more expensive boats, with impressive superstructures, awnings and fishing gear.

*The top end of the market.*

As befits a port of entry or disembarkation, the entire scene is not as tranquil as you might expect. There is a hint of industry, only dialled back a bit. This is not the London docks or Hamburg. I can see bustle along the walkways, and in a service area of offices; even a supermarket with jacked up prices. People scratch their heads at a chandlery store and marine repair, and ponder fixes to dings and bashes received on voyages. Others prepare to slip anchor for Caribbean sailing further afield.

As we glide into the berth, a small reception committee briskly walks up the jetty to meet us, including an older gentleman wearing a yellow t-shirt with a clipboard under one arm. His other arm is missing—it ends in a hook.

He stands with a delighted beam on his round, and slightly chubby face, clipboard clasped to his chest. He asks for a declaration.

"Well done, you made it," he pronounces—"Can we have your time, please."

Knut references a note in his hand and announces in deliberate English:

"Eighteen days, three hours and 21 minutes."

This is on par for the size of our boat. We've done well taking in to account the boats in the fleet—many who are not racing, and are content to take their time.

We gingerly step, one by one, over on to the jetty.

*This is really bizarre.*

The days at sea and the acquisition of sea-legs mean we now sway down the boardwalk, having become accustomed to the roll and yaw of *Derelict*. It's strange to be on such stable land, and it takes some getting used to. We now need to jettison our sea legs and re-acquire the lost land ones we put away temporarily.

I gaze around the marina and to the verdant hills that provide protection from offshore winds coming in from the sea. There are little houses dotted on the nearby hills, valleys and shoreline.

*Where do these people work? Do they spend their lives at light work, retiring to a hammock in the late afternoon, drinking Pimms at nightfall?*

I glance at our neighbours, yachties from The Netherlands and Switzerland, and I'm most impressed that the Swiss can be such ocean farers. The Dutch are a youngish crowd, no one over 30, and an athletic blonde girl wanders around in a royal blue one-piece swimsuit, calling out in her native tongue to her friends. We suck our stomachs in and stand straighter when she comes over to say "Hi".

"We have been here two days," she tells us. "Got to tell you– there's a sea beach across the bay–a little bus takes you there."

She says this with a delightful characteristic Dutch lisp and guttural nuance. The Swiss, whilst friendly, are quieter and keep themselves to themselves.

I get talking to the man with the hook who greeted us. He's a former British Army brigadier called Boris. He's with a small yacht *Warrior*, and is cruising with the sons of friends, connections in his wide and elaborate social network. I glance at his missing arm without being too blatant about it. It's truncated at the elbow—and he carries the stump across his chest most of the time unconsciously.

*I wonder what happened.* It's too soon to enquire.

Later, when I pass *Warrior*, in a daze, I say hello. A pair of floppy-haired, well-spoken English boys on deck greet me, both in their early twenties. They introduce themselves.

"I'm Howard," the first says.

He is tall, about six foot, with curls.

"I'm Larry," say the other.

He's about the same height, but slimmer. They introduce me too two ladies from the organising committee who are leaning against the rail. Howard has taken a liking to one and announces he'd love to marry a girl like her one day, which makes her blush and laugh.

There are other essentials. We file down the jetty in our sandals and flip-flops, and head to the shower block, towels and wash bags under our arm. It's grand to soap up, taking our time, and luxuriate in the hot freshwater and suds cascading down our bodies after being cooped up at sea. We wash our clothes and underwear in the sinks and wring the grey water out of them, taking a turn around the plumbing to twist the water out. Jurgen sings German Bundesliga football songs.

We waddle down to the bar and restaurant at the marina's end. After well-deserved rounds of lager and slices of pizza, though, conversation slows and our heads droop, and we've all got one thing on our mind—a good night's sleep—with no watch.

## 40 BAR AND GRILL

It feels strange to wake to the low-key noise of the marina when we've become accustomed to only the sounds of *Derelict* running before the wind, bird calls, and that same wind in the rigging; perhaps a low conversation in the cabin. We allow ourselves a bit of a lie in, but I wake and stretch by 8 am, excited to be somewhere new.

We have bacon and eggs and fresh *espresso* coffee in a little café across the street from the marina, enjoying the morning sun, which slants in below the umbrellas, across the week-old international newspapers and reflects off our breakfast plates.

"This is great, eh?" I tell Simon. "Pass me the *International Express* mate."

Rik plans to visit Reduit beach, that sea beach on the bay—it runs for a kilometre parallel with the marina. Before it gets hot, we head over to have a look. The minibus we were told about ferries people from the marina the long way around by a track. We pay with local currency and stand in the aisle, as all the seats are occupied.

We head off with our rolled towels, and waddle like amateurs in our flip-flops on to the golden sands and take in the view. It's a skinny littoral, chopped-up with foot traffic at our end, flattening out to pristine sand worn flat by the sea's rollers at the other.

We pad past lines of recliners all pretty in a row. We hear the shouted voices and glee of swimmers out in the shallows, brought to us on a breeze. Yachts are moored further out, and there's a jet ski and parascending outfit taking punters.

"Any sharks, mate?" I ask Rik playfully.

He is pretty sure there are no sharks here.

*It will do nicely.*

All I am missing now is a rum and Coke. And there's no sign of James Bond's Ursula Andress from *Dr No* emerging from the water either.

*This is Saint Lucia, though, not Jamaica—wrong island.*

There's a choice of ends. At one, a resort, with a leisure centre, or the quieter southern end? We choose the southern end. Dropping towels to secure our territory, we see a large, forested hill, Mount Pimard, and a sign-posted trail leads there. A hill walk or parascending?

It's another easy decision, and not long later, I find myself in the shade of a palm tree approaching the parascending business operator.

"You ready to fly?" he asks.

He must say this hundreds of times a day. I nod in the affirmative, and listen to the safety brief from one of his offsiders, a relaxed dude. It's not long later when I'm being pulled behind the boat in the shallows before becoming airborne —whooping with excitement, looking down at the bay.

It's time to head back to change. Boats are still making their way in from the Atlantic. Each vessel is welcomed to Rodney Bay with rum punches from a platter, a basket of fresh fruit and chilled beer. No matter what time of day or night, the welcoming committee is waiting. I see a sign:

*Presentation and live music on the boardwalk tonight*

*The boardwalk.* Bruce Willis comes to mind.

At dusk, we stand around at the marina manager's cocktail party and clap deserved winners of prizes, and endure a few speeches, adopting polite expressions. We pay close attention to the trays borne aloft by waiters. There's also a lot of in-jokes and references most of us don't get. We see Jimmy from the daily radio call—he remembers me, and comments on my discipline. Rik catches my eye, and we're happy to slip away to the bars once the headline presentations are over.

I am strolling through the marina the next day and recognise Larry and Howard from *Warrior* at the bar having a drink: they drag a chair out for me to sit down on, and I join them while

"Wonderwall" from Oasis plays on the speakers.

I glance at the middle-aged yachties here—all polo tops and deck shoes, with hairy, bandy calves and degrees of sunburn and established tans. I hear Home Counties Received Pronunciation English and northern accents, as well as French and German. In a grassy area overlooking the bay, children play, running around. Every now and again, their mums look up from their *New York Times Bestseller* books to check their charges.

Boris joins us, sitting next to me, dressed in the same yellow top that he was wearing when I first met him. We start with small talk, then he tells me about his service. When Larry and Howard are out of earshot, he explains his arm,

"We were patrolling in Belfast back in the 1980s when we were ambushed by a sniper—he shot me through the radius and destroyed it. The surgery was moderately successful, Steve, but I received a nasty infection, and they took it off below the elbow."

He went on to a perfectly normal service career, commanded his regiment, and retired to a life at home in the wilds of rural Dorset, to do the *Telegraph* crossword, and cruise the world with his boat. And, it turns out Howard is the son of a Lord of the Realm—I make a note to look him up in *Burke's Peerage* when I get back.

Larry comes back with a round of drinks for us all.

"Hello Skipper," he says agreeably. "You having a drink?"

Boris rubs his stump furiously, as is his habit, and declines. It's a "no, thank you" today.

"Okay Skipper, just looking after you."

After Boris leaves, the three of us order another beer. At about 7 pm, the music is turned up a notch, and we speak louder to make ourselves heard. The middle-aged crew have all slipped away back to their families, leaving those with rather more addled livers behind to plot, and a younger crowd has arrived to enjoy a drink—girls in sarongs, and boys in t-shirts and Hawaiian shirts.

A man arrives and sets up a karaoke machine. A gaggle of teenage girls wait nearby for their chance, the older ones stirring their Pina Coladas furiously to pass the time before they can have a sing.

"One more, lads," announces Howard.

We toast our good fortunes out here in the tropics. The surroundings of the marina are sort of swimming, and I can't see into the distance as well as I could earlier this afternoon. I stumble back to *Derelict*, to the strains of "I will Survive" blaring from the speakers.

# 41 IT'S CAPITAL

*A ship in harbour is safe, but that is not what ships are built for.*
John Shedd

Christmas is not so far away, now, and I can imagine the angst and build-up back in the UK—TV adverts, the count-down of shopping days left, and conversation turning to the likelihood of snow on Christmas Day, even if that's just a snowflake. Before long, it will be all over, and the UK will emerge the other side into the depths of winter. Life in the Caribbean, in the dry season, is far more straightforward. We have all gone on to tropical time readily.

It would be too easy to lounge around in the perhaps insular marina (and it is) talking to new-found friends, sipping gin and tonics, with ice. We could muse about what to do in the afternoon and what to do tomorrow. As for light refreshment, "The sun is always over the yard-arm." In all honesty, there is either a little something to do, or not much to do at all.

We look at the posted evening entertainment and make small trips as tourists. Not many yachties want to leave the marina, they are content to sit on board and talk to new acquaintances berthed nearby. I can just imagine my parents wouldn't be impressed if I was to sit in the marina all day, so I decide to venture further afield. I figure my liver will appreciate it, too.

Castries, the capital, is an hour away along the Gros Inlet-Castries Highway, and there's a minibus by way of public transport that winds its way along tarmac roads, and dirt tracks just wide enough. The driver obligingly provides entertainment by way of reggae tracks from his radio, and I can spot the passengers swaying to the music—or more likely—due to the ruts and corrugations of the road. We pass through local villages which have some life with kids playing in the streets. Everyone seems happy.

Trees with gigantic fronds soar above the road. In the hills, I can see orchids where mangoes, bananas and avocados grow for export. The average Saint Lucian is poor in world terms, and the tourist dollar goes far—we are in a third-world country after all. The local currency is the East Caribbean Dollar, about three of them to the US dollar, so prices seem expensive to those that go by the pound Sterling.

Many of the houses we pass by are double-storey, each one painted in a different colour—pink, baby-blue and yellow. Most have verandahs upstairs, overlooking the road, and to the rear overlooking a coterie of animals. Many are raised above the ground so that cooling breezes can fan underneath—and there is space for a car port below instead of a garage. Pickup trucks are popular to get around in. The roofs are often metal to protect better from rampant bad weather.

As we approach the town from the outskirts, (I've read it has a population of about 15,000) I can see quite a panorama in the bay and a gigantic cruise ship in harbour. We find ourselves on the streets downtown, I figure I'll get off when everyone else does. Our driver pulls over at the stop serving the town centre, so I find myself standing in the street alone whilst everyone else with business to get on with hurries off.

I stride into the post office, feeling like Sean Connery in *Dr No*, (only I'm not in a suit, and there are many other differences). I find salacious postcards to mail friends and find others for family. There's a supermarket next door. I have difficulty recognising brands and dawdle over purchases. It's not like Tesco back in the UK, and I wander the aisles having a good look. The distracted young girl near the door on the till, with braids in her hair, examines her nails. Each time she makes a sale, she wakes from her stupor and chatters briefly, displaying perfect white teeth, before resuming her inspection.

A narrow thoroughfare passes through the town, with timber buildings either side; but no awning, however, to provide any shade. Metal bollards line the streets. Power poles are placed at intervals: wires snake out to buildings in a tangle, decorated with flags. Road signs look like UK signs, but a sign depicting a skirted woman and child designate crossing places.

Next, I pop into a bookstore to find something to read—most of the books are in English thankfully. Behind one counter, I find a large man wearing glasses who beams at everyone who enters. I open a battered copy of a Caribbean book by VS Naipal.

I climb a hill on the town outskirts in time for a sudden squall to arrive. Women out shopping erect umbrellas and lean into the wind, splashing through puddles. One woman, with billowing skirts, struggles to get to cover and settles for damp hair, which she fixes up with a pin, grinning at me. The rain stops as fast as it begins, and the sun comes out once more: the humidity though, is a constant—and I'm sweating into my cotton t-shirt. Just as well it's not September, the wettest time of year when eight inches of water fall in the gauge. At least we're in the cooler parts of the year.

I'm overdue for a late afternoon meal, seeing as I missed lunch. I want to try local fare, so choose a restaurant by the side of the road, where a proprietor cooks and serves to order.

I consider the green figs (bananas) I can see on the menu. The figs, boiled and sautéed with peppers, herbs and spices sound delicious, but I play it safe and settle for Catch of the Day.

Full, and feeling like Bill Bryson now, I saunter into the King George the Fifth gardens, and my eyes veer off the tidy paths and manicured lawns to the brush.

*Are there any snakes?*

I've read the Fer de-lance is the only venomous snake on the island. I'm hoping I won't see one. There's a funny little two-storey house painted pink with a turret, and a domed cupola up top with a viewing platform.

It's a hike, but I chance the walk-to La Toc Beach. By the time I reach the fine sands, I've acquired a nasty little blister. I can access the beach through the grounds of a swish resort. The wait staff don't mind me plopping down at a table and ordering an ice-cold coke—then another.

I don't fancy the return walk, so hail a taxi back to the bus stop. I have all the time in the world, so prop up against the wall and gaze around at fellow passengers queuing for the return to Gros Inlet.

Back at the marina, slower yachts are still coming in from their Atlantic crossing, some with kids and teens. Larry and Howard say "Hi"s when I saunter past, limping with my blister, and I stop briefly to chat.

I straddle the railing back on *Derelict*, and the crew can see I've been having a chat with my English compatriots. I have a sneaking suspicion this irritates them—that there is a question mark over my loyalties.

"Steve!"

Knut approaches me and presents me with a piece of paper.

Taking it in hand, I see it's an invoice. It has my name on the top left corner, and the amount due in the bottom right corner is 2,000 US dollars.

"It's for costs. You pay please!" implores Knut, pointing out the grand total for emphasis.

These are itemized expenses, I can see, and this takes a while to sink in. My eye catches:

*Steering mechanism*
*Labour*

I frown.
*What's this? How the hell am I going to pay this?*

## 42 TIME TO JUMP SHIP

"**I**t's for the charter," Knut reinforces.

*The charter.*

"We have to repair the rudder," he says.

The damage we incurred near Barbados, and for a bunch of sundry expenses, too, by the looks of it.

The penny drops. It dawns on me, that all along, I was not a bona fide crew member in the normal sense of the word, but I had come across as a member of a charter, and that means I am on the hook for boat repairs incurred during that hire.

This fact sinks in, whilst my brain races for a way out.

"Knut, I'm a crew member. I didn't hire the boat, I paid my way, paid for food and expenses," I insist. "I have no means of paying Knut. I'm not liable," I add.

Knut is not easily swayed. He's looking a little aggressive and won't back down yet.

"You signed," he says, widening his stance and jutting his chin forward.

*Signed?*

"Look!" he emphasises.

He turns on his heel to the shelving behind the radio looking for the paperwork he claims to have presented to me back in the Canaries. There's a hesitancy in his actions, and he scratches his head—and I think it dawns on us both at the same time.

*I didn't sign any paperwork. And he knows it.*

"I don't recall signing, Knut. Can you show me?" I ask.

*I can sense the tide has turned.*

It's obvious he was so distracted with us being in dry dock on the day I arrived that he simply forgot to ask for my signature.

"*Scheisse.*"

He swears under his breath, departing from High German for the moment. Realising he doesn't have a leg to stand on, he turns back towards me, grips my arm and points:

"You go. You leave!"

The others hear his raised voice and glance up. I'm not so worried, even relieved, now I'm off the hook. It is no skin off my nose, so under the awkward gaze of the others, I head to the bunk to retrieve my pack and belongings. As I am used to living out of a suitcase, it doesn't take long. I nod briefly at Jurgen, who struggles to maintain his gaze.

I hop across the railing for the last time and step out on to the jetty.

*How do I feel?*

I'm footloose and fancy free, time for a change in any case.

Along the boardwalk, out of earshot, I bump into Simon coming back to *Derelict* after an errand. He peers at me.

"What's with the pack, mate? Going somewhere?" he asks.

"Well, did you cough up for those 'expenses'," Simon?" I ask him.

He looks irritated.

"Certainly did, Steve. I signed–I chartered the boat for my holiday down here. It was made clear to me in that paperwork. I figured in the Canaries we weren't just crewing after all."

I explain as per my call with Knut earlier on in the year, that I thought we had a crewing arrangement—after all, I had put my name down on a crewing list in the first place.

"Well done, mate, on getting out of that one," he replies.

"I'll work something out accommodation wise to take me through to Christmas, Simon."

We shake on it, and I wish him all the luck. He scurries back to *Derelict*, looking a bit dejected. I feel sorry for the way things turned out for him, sick as he is.

Backpack over my shoulder, I walk down the jetty, approaching *Warrior*. Boris is ferreting in the cockpit, peering overboard at passersby, and looks pleased to see me. I explain my situation, and he rubs his stump in consternation with a bothered look on his flushed face.

"That is not on, Steve, that's not how it's supposed to work.

You are a crew member. Money should not be changing hands at all. I'm glad you're not on the hook for that one."

He does, however, have an immediate suggestion which pleases me no end;

"Would you like to come sailing with us? We've got a spare berth. I'll ask you to contribute to food and basic expenses, that's all."

"I'd love to, Boris," I reply.

I can barely believe my luck. I would have been in a backpackers' otherwise until it was time to return to the UK.

The boys look delighted, and I throw up my pack, climb up, and find a spare berth for'ard, again in the bow, my habitual spot.

"Steve, want to come for a spin in the dinghy?" asks Larry. "I'm heading out."

The dinghy is tied alongside the boat, and we clamber in, and Larry sits at the stern, hand on tiller. I find a bench and sit amidships. We untie mooring lines and Larry pulls hard on the starter rope of the outboard. The 40 brake horse power engine starts in only a couple of pulls, and smiling, he steers us out in to the marina. He closes the choke, and we motor past yachts greeting people we've got to know.

"Right, let's head out and along the sea beach," he says.

Once away from the moorings, Larry cranks open the throttle, and the bow comes up and we plane through the water around the bay to the beach. I shift my seat to balance the boat better. We careen up the shore a hundred metres off the surf, to one end of the bay and then circle for another run back. Little kids wave at us, and parents look up. Larry has a wicked look on his face.

"One more," he cries.

*Yup.*

Back at *Warrior*, Boris and Howard are waiting for us and there's supper left over from yesterday.

It's a pleasure being with this new crew, honestly. They are quick-witted, fun, and friendly. Nothing is a problem, nothing is too hard, all good blokes to a tee. Boris tells me about his sailing. He and Howard came down from Boston on the Eastern seaboard of the US, heading south past Miami, having flown into the US. Larry joined from Newport near Washington.

Boris adds, "I didn't make the Atlantic crossing with *Warrior*. She was crewed by friends in the club for me. They've gone on to Barbados now. I did it a few times in my thirties when I was on leave. I don't find it that interesting."

The club he refers to is the Royal Yacht Squadron, and Boris looks over his shoulder at the white flag flying from the back.

"White is for *Royal boats* such as the Royal Yacht Britannia, which flies a White Ensign. Blue is reserved only for Royal Navy vessels, as you may have noticed."

"Now you mention it, they are blue, Boris," I reply.

"Every other vessel registered in the UK flies the Red Ensign."

I hadn't noticed that.

As for the sail south from the United States:

"It's a much more challenging cruise, Stephen, more interesting anyway," he says. "The wind direction shifts around more, and the weather is less settled at this time of year."

*I can well believe him.*

## 43 GONNA NEED A BIGGER BOAT

**D**ays go by in the marina. Everyone is now on Caribbean time, with not much to worry about at all, only where the next meal will come from, and how we'll while away the hours until the evening brings welcome coolness. The weather is agreeable, not too hot though, with a hint of humidity. Hurricane season is well over, and the climate will be stable until the northern spring at least.

There's an expat community in the bay. The long timers have a nonchalance, not fazed by the allure of the tropics.

We explore the local bars and restaurants. Many are simple affairs sort of in the Mexican mold, tin shacks with white-washed bricks and awnings for shade, with counters, behind which owners prepare snacks and drinks, turning a profit on the tourist markup. In lieu of a menu, most have displays of colas and lemonades with cheap plastic tables and chairs set out. Others are more sophisticated with waiter service.

Larry, Howard and I visit one up the hill from Gros Inlet. There's a bloke sitting here who Larry has met before.

"Meet Martin," he says.

He is sitting cross-legged, smoking a cigarette with a collection of notes and coins on the counter in front of him. He's wearing a grubby t-shirt, flip-flops, and has two-day stubble, overdue for a haircut maybe. Martin's even a bit grungy. He is not a big man, and has a bit of a distended belly, as befits someone who doesn't pay a great deal of attention to diet or exercise, but budgets for drink and smokes. He holds out his hand, takes a drag on his cigarette, and sizes me up.

"Which boat are you with," I ask.

"Oyster," Howard says, answering for him.

I know this boat. *It's a big boat.*

*Oyster Bay* is a large 60-foot ketch I've seen. I've come to recognize boats moored up in the marina as I've traipsed the boards.

"That's quite a boat, Martin," I comment, taking a sip of beer, noting it's warming up already.

"Not mine, though," he replies. "I'm skipper. I'm looking after it for the owner."

"Right," I say.

It turns out he's baby-sitting this yacht and has brought her down from Miami.

"My client is off in the US working, but will arrive in Saint Lucia to join later in the New Year. I've got to get her ready for sail. I'll be skippering for the owner," he explains.

What's more, he explains he sailed her on his own from Florida past Cuba down here.

"I used the automatic steering vane so I could sleep and cook."

Long before I had heard of the international rich and the likes of the Russians, this seems like unfathomable wealth, and a lifestyle I can't comprehend. It appears a different world away from the UK and London. Martin is house-sitting a floating home.

We chat for an hour. Martin comes over as droll and doesn't seem to get in a flap about anything, but this demeanor turns out to hide an enquiring intellect and ease.

We finish our beers, and it's my turn to settle the bill. I refuse to take payment from Martin when he pushes a few notes across the table. He rolls another cigarette, licking the paper with sideways motion of his head.

We saunter out of the bar, flipping our sunglasses off our heads down over our eyes and walk back down to the marina, taking our time.

"Come and walk with me, I'll show you *Oyster*," he says, and we take a left, rather than the right I'd take to get to *Warrior*.

*Oyster Bay* takes pride of place in the top end of the marina, painted white below the waterline and English mustard yellow above with two masts, and she rises and falls against her moorings lazily. She's a fair bit more impressive than the two yachts I've sailed on so far, in fact, quite a bit more.

Martin steps through a gap in the rail and strides down the deck with aplomb, and I follow. The ladder, which seems to go on forever from an equipment-laden cockpit, descends to a lovely saloon area artfully fitted out. She's a cut above the boats I have been on so far. This is the top end of town, where luxury lives cheek by jowl with the utility you'd expect on a boat.

The entire cabin is decked out in tasteful wood mahogany, with metal accents—I can smell the money. There's a built-in blond, wooden bookcase over a comfy looking padded lounge seat next to a table.

I go for'ard and find a generous master bedroom raised on a mezzanine, bigger than my room back home. I duck my head around the door, and there's a sleeping bag strewn on the double mattress suiting someone who doesn't want to make a bed. Like me, it looks like Martin is inclined to live out of a suitcase on the move. His life would be a nomadic one, at the beck and call of owners and agencies. It must be a fascinating life though, with lots of different ports to visit.

I pass my eye over the living area. On the bookshelf: a copy of the *Cruising Guide*, *Blue Water Sailing* and *The Firm* by John Grisham. A little TV and a sparse collection of video tapes—the *Lion King* pokes out of the VCR, half-ejected. Martin lights yet another cigarette and picks a Pepsi from a fitted refrigerator, and looks at me, eyebrows raised.

"What do you reckon, Steve?" he says eventually.

"Very nice," I shrug. "I could get used to this."

As I step back down the ladder, Martin grabs the rail, but slips and bumps into me. My wallet is knocked out of my hip pocket below the swell of the marina into the silt at the bottom. I can't say I will miss the wallet, but I'll struggle without my credit card —my funds are gone.

*Bugger.* My mind races.

"Shit, I've lost my credit card," I say, to state the obvious.

Martin, keen to make amends, helps me look: we study the waters. They are a bit murky. A small launch with scuba divers comes by. Martin suggests that maybe a diver can look for it, so we hail them, explaining my situation. One of them, an Englishman, agrees to dive once he's taken a break. They tie up alongside, and he takes sips out of a bottle of chilled water.

"OK, let's take a look," he says.

He comes over with a spare tank, not 100 per cent kitted out, and slips into the water at the stern, not even bothering with fins. He's down for a few minutes, surfaces, gives me a thumbs down—bad news—and then dives again. Surfacing again with an update, he slips below once more. After this is unproductive, we agree that it's a lost cause.

"Sorry, man, that's about all I can do," he says.

I thank him, nonetheless, and he leaves us and motors away down the marina.

Luckily, I have several hundreds of dollars stashed down the bottom of my sleeping bag, and all my accommodation, food and transport organised and paid for, so I think I can handle this little drama.

I am flagging a bit over marina life and running out of things to do. I am beginning to wonder if there's enough to keep the average person active, and chastise myself for an uncustomary bout of negativity. Martin comes to my aid.

We sit onboard *Oyster*, and, over a beer, he tells me about the various places he has crewed and stories from his time at sea which perks me up. We don't find the solution for world peace entirely, but we do put the world to rights. One beer turns to another, and we ask each other through his cigarette smoke to repeat sentences so we can both follow the myriad threads of our conversation. He talks about his beginnings in Southampton near the water.

"I grew up with it, Steve. It's been my life."

We stagger to the Friday night street party and join in, not wanting to pass up the opportunity. There are people selling a medley of local seafood and delicacies. We halt at stands and sample local beers and strong rum punches. Music plays reggae loudly on repeat.

Martin has a cigarette in hand, and sways when the music stops, missing the beat. It's a fusillade of sound and it goes on into the early hours, long after I'm sound asleep on board a 60 feet yacht, crashed out on the luxurious leather couch.

## 44 A GRAND TIME

**K**nowing Martin brings benefits—he seems to know everyone around the marina and is on first-name terms with the shop owners and staff. It's the sort of bloke he is. I see him getting on with everyone as he comes and goes on errands.

One day we are at the bar, and we are joined by an acquaintance, Ian. He lives out here with his parents who have retired—his father used to work at the UK consulate in Castries. They maintain a villa here, the best time to lie low away from the wintry blasts of the Atlantic. Martin says artfully, playing the man:

"So, Ian–when are we getting an invite to your place?"

"Tomorrow. Come over tomorrow," replies Ian. "You too, Steve. Larry, Howard."

"Good one. I'm tired of the marina," replies Martin. "What about you, Steve?"

"Yeah, I'll come, I'm up for it," I reply.

"Okay, I'll pick you up, before lunch, right after I've been to town. Crash over for the night."

Ian drives everywhere in a late model 1980s Essex-girl-white Golf GTI cabriolet—still all the rage—the top concertinaed and folded down like oversized bellows, and he heads off, with a burble from the exhaust.

There's opportunity for an omelette the next day whilst we wait for him. By the time Ian pulls up, Martin is tipsy from our little breakfast already, having started on the grog, and Ian greets us from the driving seat. Martin chooses the passenger seat and puts his bare, calloused and brown feet up on the dash and juts his elbow out on the door. He positions his hat just right using the wing mirror. We squeeze in the back, and before long, we are driving along winding roads up into the hills overlooking

Castries, making us feel queasy as we take the bends. If the roof was up, we'd bang our heads as the Golf hits ruts on the tarmacadam roads.

"Watch out for the torque steer, Ian," murmurs Larry.

In a while, we get to an angled turnoff. Ian takes it sharply, in a flurry of gravel, and we are scrunching down a road with villas on either side. There's seclusion behind gates—no one to be seen anywhere, not even a maintenance worker.

At the end of the road, the land continues to climb into lush countryside. A path snakes into it; maybe there's camping up there. This end is more exclusive, and we find an open gate with a security booth and a bored-looking guard. He recognises Ian, and salutes as we drive through. Ian returns it nonchalantly.

"Cheers," he murmurs.

There are two houses on both sides of this cul-de-sac and we halt at one. At a gate, Ian leans out and keys a PIN into a keypad and the gate slides open on ball-bearings. He stops in the driveway at the front door of a villa. He kills the engine. Looking around, we note a small fountain currently not flowing, and a little shed for security.

"We don't have security at the moment," remarks our host. "Nothing ever happens," he adds.

We follow him to a brick patio. I expect to see a butler at the door, but none materialises.

We can see a tidy lawn with stripes cut into it, which slopes gently to an orchard. There's an orange Husqvarna ride on mower parked in a small shed, nose out, with a backpack of glyphosate resting on the seat. Larry admires a landscaped swimming pool with clear water, an exquisite tiled surround, leaves floating on the surface and some resting on the bottom. He tries a recliner set out higgledy-piggledy, with a leaf pole across the armrests.

"Nice pad," comments Howard. "You've got quite the place here, mate," he adds, hands on hips, nodding.

The house is large and an architect design, with laid out gardens. It looks like a cross between a neo-Gothic and Georgian design, but I'm no student of architecture. The patio abuts French windows, which gives us views into a corpulent interior. To my eye, maybe it's Hamptons, but I am not an interiors expert either.

We have a quick wander on the ground floor, where we duck into an open-plan kitchen. I crane through a doorway into a study with bay windows granting views to the lawn.I see a large partner's desk with green leather inserts, and there are books lined up on bespoke fitted shelves. We don't go upstairs. A chandelier overlooks twin carpeted staircases that circle up to the landing. I suppose you could keep one for best and use the other.

Out on the patio, we flop into wicker garden chairs and wonder what to do next.

Martin, who has been here before, offers us a drink from a bar fridge built into a feature wall.

"Help yourselves, lads, we've stocked up," Ian says.

I get a bottle of lager and twist a slice of lemon into it, making up a lager top, as if I am in a busy boozer in South London. Ian makes himself a Martini, expertly squeezing an olive around the glass. Martin lights a cigarette and with it poised between his lips, he tilts over and accepts a Corona.

"Lovely."

He splits a bag of peanuts and arranges them for people to help themselves, removing his flip-flops. He offers his hand to a Jack Russell dog, which has appeared, who licks the salt off his fingers before curling up at his feet.

We chat more, shooting the breeze. It's great to be home somewhere after living aboard for the best part of a month. I stretch my feet out and dangle my hands over the armrests of the chair.

The sun has been over the patio roof and for 20 minutes, it streams into our happy little group before careening for the horizon. At sunset, we watch the blob of incandescent light as the sun squeezes its way down for the night. Howard calls out,

"Cheers," and we chink our bottles and glasses contently.

Ian's sister, and her friend, back from a shopping trip.

"Hey guys. How's it going?" one says.

"This is my sister," Ian says, getting up.

She is about 25, slim and lithe, with muscular and well-turned calves. Her friend Kate is taller, with a brunette fringe which frames her face. Ian's sister nips inside and comes back with a handful of CDs.

"Boys, let's change the music," she implores. "You've got no taste."

She pokes her brother in the ribs. He shrugs.

"I'm SO bored," she announces, and she accepts a drink from her dad's supply.

"What are you guys doing... This is MY house. Dad's not back 'til Wednesday."

"Chill out," Ian says. "We're cool."

We listen to music, a bit of Oasis, and Alanis Morissette. Kate lights a spliff and passes it around the group. Meanwhile, the cicadas chirp around us.

*God, this is good.*

The world starts to spin; a potent mix of beer and spirits has hit me. Kate speaks now and exhales slowly.

"Let's go out," she says to no one in particular. "Need to DO something. I'm SO bored," she repeats.

"I'll call transport," Ian says.

# 45 NIGHT OUT

The next hours pass in a blur. A local man who helps out around the house and gardens turns up in a little minibus (he runs people to and from town when he's not doing odd jobs in the place.) There is space for us all, and he takes us into town along the ruts again, but this time we don't notice them. Ian follows behind in the GTI preferring his independence.

We head into an expats' bar, yet another place where people wind down the clock. We sip cocktails and feel heady and in a good mood. It's grand to be away from the marina and the families, and with a younger crowd. There's a reggae band in the corner and they've got the volume cranked up. A trio of local men with sunglasses crack out reggae and other well-known numbers.

We drink Martinis, Daiquiris, Manhattans, combinations with Baileys; Mexican Coronas served with salt which Ian shows us, unaware of how cliched his behaviour is. I get chatting to Kate and lean closer to hear what she is saying over the noise of the band.

"My life is so f**ked," she says to me.

I look sympathetic.

"Why's that, Kate?" I ask.

"I'm so tired with it. Saint Lucia is so boring. I have a friend in Cayman, it's so much better. Not many young people here. Dad is always away."

I sympathise. I can't imagine a life out here after life in London. What's worse? She accepts a cigarette from Martin, who has leant in, flicking his ash into a tray that the barmaid slips under his arm. She tells me that she doesn't have a boyfriend, but she likes dancing at the local bars.

At about 2am, Kate says,

"Let's go."

We leave the bar and chat in the street.

It's beautifully mild, after the warmth of the day and the humidity has dropped out of the sky. There are not many people around. Most of the locals were in bed long ago as they get up early. Ian's had a drink or two, eased up, had a few more; but he convinced he's still good to drive—he reckons the local police are relaxed about it. He pulls up, windows open, and we order a taxi to take us all back.

We get back safely along the winding roads with the cool night breeze wafting in, waking us up, with the cabrio flapping.

We flop on to sofas in the living room in front of a state-of-the-art rear projection TV. We sit and chat—Martin has his bare feet up again on the coffee table and busies himself rolling yet another cigarette. Someone puts on a CD and adjusts the volume. Kate gets a coffee from the kitchen, turns to me and says conversationally,

"Do you want to come up," and leads the way upstairs.

I walk up behind her, swaying with the drink, following her up the stairs to a landing where several bedrooms lead off, hitting the banister twice. This room is dark, full of soft toys and teddy bears—she dismisses them with a flourish of her hand.

"Oh…don't worry about those."

*I'm not.*

I wake up the next morning, fuzzy-headed and confused. I can't work out where I am for a while, London? and there's no water rushing past a hull either. It dawns on me eventually, and I tilt my head and see Kate. She's fast asleep, on her back, snoring like a bunny rabbit. I hunt down the landing for the bathroom, and jump in the shower and turn on the hot water. I dry off with a towel I find in a cabinet, feeling one-hundred per cent better already. I creep downstairs. A maid is in the kitchen emptying the rubbish bins, and indicates the cooktop without a word. There's bacon and eggs sizzling in a pan on the hob.

Martin is standing on a little patio near the French doors looking out at the pool. He looks calm, and he regards me, his morning rollup in hand, ashtray tactically positioned on a pot plant just in reach.

"OK, Steve, how did you sleep, mate?"

"Yeah, all right. My head hurts." He nods.

The boys come down a bit later and Howard rubs his hands and smells the bacon rashers which have now crisped up nicely.

"You'd like some?" says the maid.

"Lovely, please," Howard replies, cheekily.

The maid serves up grapefruit juice in a jar from the refrigerator and I wince as the sugar hits.

*Loving it.*

The egg is cooked to perfection and oozes yolk. The coffee hits the spot.

Feeling more alive, we go and sit cross-legged out on the lawn in the shade as the sun climbs up the sky. Kate talks about her life in Europe, her skirt tight across her thighs, her hair loose, running her painted nails through her hair.

Larry spots a chess set in the study and brings it over, cradling it.

"Anyone for a game?"

We relax as the sun continues its trajectory, its rays shortening the shady area we have sought out shelter in. Its warmth teases us, making us feel better and waking us up bit by bit. We stretch our limbs, allowing the light to play on our toes.

Ian runs us back down the hill to the marina before what would be a good time for a late lunch. Boris is busy reading the *Daily Telegraph,* which he has got from the marina supplies, and raises his eyebrows when we step on-board.

"Okay boys, I'm ready, I've worked it out. This is the plan–we're heading south to Bequia tomorrow. How about spending Christmas there? It's quieter, a bit off the beaten track."

"Sounds great," says Howard.

Larry and I nod in agreement. Bequia is past Saint Vincent. I can get back to Saint Lucia easily enough for my UK flight.

"It's a straight-forward sail, easy enough. Oh, Howard–I spoke to your father–he's well, but he's off to New York next week. Didn't speak to yours, Larry, sure he's ok, though. Did you contact your parents?" he asks me.

He turns his attention to the crossword puzzle, and I peer over his shoulder and supply him with suggestions.

We nip over to the supermarket and stock up with fresh food; bananas and apples, oranges and tomatoes, ripe bell peppers, and a chocolate cake as a treat. The lady at the till holds out her hand, and I give Boris cash to cover it. He buys a new pair of flip-flops and discards his old pair, dropping them in a street bin where they land with a muted thud. He slaps back to *Warrior*, *Financial Times* under an arm, and we three follow with the shopping.

# 46 SAILING SOUTH

Time to slip our moorings, then, after a good portion of time spent in Rodney Bay. It's another glorious day with a breeze in the Windward chain. This early, the marina is at its most quiet apart from other crews arranging to depart to destinations up and down the chain. We're turning left, towards Central America.

Once again, I'm with a new crew, on a new boat and again— the most junior member, but that doesn't faze me. At least I have several weeks at sea under my belt now.

Boris takes the wheel, and Larry and Howard adopt practised positions—Skipper indicates where I can perch for our departure. Larry unpeels the mooring line from the last bollard and throws it inboard, leaping on to the deck. Howard and I push off. We chug along the marina, past the fleet and the crews going about their business. There's a sailor up a mast of a 50-footer, feet in stirrups, safety rope attached, with a helper belaying him. Looks like repairs or inspection of the masthead.

As we cross the bay into the Caribbean, we cop the wind blowing southerly, so we will be running downwind. With a grimace of concentration, Boris spins the wheel over, and we run the sails up quickly and they tighten. The breeze brings with it the smell of the sea, mixed in with shore smells.

Boris confirms today's plan—he wants to sail south to a choice beach at Anse Chastanet. We'll go past the Pitons, a well-known feature on the southern end of Saint Lucia. They are two mountainous volcanic plugs that rise to steep spires overlooking the sea. They are known as Gros Piton and Petit Piton, both under 800 metres high. That's about three-quarters the height of Mount Snowdon in Wales. They are World Heritage Site listed, and located near the town of Soufrière. There's even a beer named after them.

One hour cruising from the marina, we pass by Marigot Bay,

perhaps a nicer place, certainly less busy than Rodney Bay. It's a narrow inlet with moorings and a tableau of palm trees at the entrance. We peer in using the binoculars as we go past—I've read about this select mooring in a sailing book.

We stop under the shadow of Jalousie Plantation for a light lunch of fresh bread, tomatoes and goat's cheese.

I ask Boris about his time in public service. He tells me that after a tour on the staff of an armoured brigade, he got a treasured appointment to the Royal Household. He was an equerry to a senior member of the Royal Family and enjoyed his time there.

"It was interesting the occasions we had to change for dinner. The Duke of Edinburgh timed us and would look at his watch when we came down, commenting on how fast or slow we had been."

He guffaws over choice stories like these he can drip-feed without creating a scandal.

"He knew how to liven things up," he chortles.

It's fascinating, and I pretend to be unmoved by the revelations he shares.

With the afternoon lengthening, we continue our track to Anse Chastanet beach. Not far from that spot, a local fisherman wearing a straw hat poles a boat towards *Warrior*. A dip of the pole in the water, and it swings alongside. He bobs up and down, peering at us, grinning, now he has our attention. He reminds me of a Gondolier in Venice. He offers us souvenirs of fruit and biscuits. We shake our heads politely.

"No thank you," Boris says assertively.

No custom today. I snap a photo of the man in the lee of the mountain—it's of *National Geographic* proportions.

Out of sight from the beach, we drift out past the mountain and Larry swims. He strips off naked, descends the ladder off the stern, his white bottom flashing, and disappears under water, head bobbing out.

"Come in Steve, it's great here," he splutters, trying not to swallow water.

We stop for the night under the shadow of a hill off the beach, pleased to be so close. Larry cooks dinner that evening, pouring boiling water from a kettle into a pan of pasta shapes, unsticking the pasta before turning to face us whilst he waits for them to cook, before serving up.

"You first, Skipper?" he asks, handing one over.

## 47 THE LIFESTYLE OF THE RICH

We lie in, festering in our sleeping bags as the cool morning turns to day. The humidity rising sees us cast them aside and get up. Boris has allowed the boat to drift closer and we can get a better look of the shoreline from the cockpit, as we wake up and munch on fruit and a yoghurt.

We make progress under sail to within about 100 metres of the shallows and drop canvas, marvelling at the sands and up at the triangular, forested Petit Piton peak (the little one) that juts out from the mainland. The walls look almost impenetrable and steep, there's no apparent way up. There's a saddle between the two hills.

Holiday makers lounge on deck chairs under trees and cabanas, and the waters of the Caribbean lap the white sands. It's a real-life picture postcard.

It's a swish place, the stuff of which I saw in the movies as a child. And it's finally the beach I have read about, thought about, and which was hitherto unattainable. It occurs to me that these people have laid out a small fortune for their accommodation and access to this resort. Now we have turned up unannounced, with nothing but a little wind debited and credited to our ledger. Boris says,

"Boys, you head off. I've got a letter to write, and a novel to get in to."

We change into our swimming trunks and manhandle our little dinghy to the stern and get in. Boris stays behind, looking content, his belly stretched over his shorts.

We paddle quietly up to the beach, allowing the surf to carry us ashore where the waters lash the sands. Larry pulls the dinghy out of the water—it's not going anywhere.

We peer up and down the shore, nodding at people who have watched our arrival from behind their sunglasses. There are small family groups. I can see fathers taking time off from the office, mothers applying suntan lotion to the neck and shoulders of their children whilst they squirm. Demure couples process down the shallows within fleeing distance to the shade, and teenage girls in bikinis promenade within safe distance of their families hoping that someone will notice them. A man dressed in shirt and trousers pushes a cart along a furrow in the sand, from which he is dispensing cans of cold drink and ice-creams. I hear an English accent, and glean the owner is a mum on her Christmas holidays.

At the far end of the beach is a small, licensed bar under a roof which provides shade, patronised by both a young and older crowd. Primary school kids sip on ice-cold Sprites, Pepsis and older gents enjoy a cocktail. Larry decides he wants a beer, and in our swimmers and t-shirts, we grab seats before they are taken.

"What are you having boys?" he asks.

"Mine's a cocktail."

I ruminate back through every movie I have ever seen, and in my mind's eye, pick one; anyone.

"A Manhattan, mate," I reply.

*Surely a Martini would be a cliché?*

"This is the life, eh, boys. Bottoms up!" Howard says, crossing one leg over the other, ankle on knee.

We chink glasses.

Feeling a little tipsy, we are noisier walking back down the sands to the dinghy, the scorching sands are less noticeable—now we've introduced ourselves to them—watched again by the mums and dads. We jump in the boat, and it rocks back and forth, and we shift about to distribute our weights before one of us tips out.

"Easy," Larry says.

He and I grab an oar each and with big strokes we head back to *Warrior* where Boris is lying on the foredeck sunbathing, a newspaper over his chest. His skin is as brown as a berry, but the rear of his neck is the shade of russet red. When we get close, he turns over on his front and waves a hand at us. As the dinghy bumps *Warrior*, he peers at us and pushes up like a cat to his knees. He holds his head at an angle and regards us.

"Guys, I reckon that dinghy is losing air," he announces. "You're low in the water, can you see?"

On closer inspection, it is confirmed: a small hole above the waterline we hadn't spotted, thankfully, a slow burn. We've made it back to *Warrior*, though.

"Well, we need to get it fixed. Let's head north, tomorrow, to Martinique. I know a chandlery there." He grimaces. "There's plenty of time."

*Great—another place to see.*

The dinghy taken up and stored, we go to action stations again. We drift past the mountain, and Howard swims, shedding clothes. He jumps into the water, head bobbing, curls trawling through the sea like a jellyfish. There's a swooping movement to my side, and Larry dives in to join him, hands clasped in front. He climbs back up the stern ladder, pausing in his nakedness. He's not shy at all.

***

We decide to climb the impressive Grand Piton peak, which rises so prominently above us. Whilst higher than Petit Piton, it's a less challenging proposition. We leave the leaking dinghy under shrub at the tree line on the shore. The route has a pleasant start on the sands, and the top looks a fair distance off. Boris knows it's climbable as he was here back in the 1980s, so we agree to chance the route. For all we know, there might be a tree or landslide blocking the path.

It is hard work, and hot work, and Howard carries a bottle of water.

We find slippery boulder fields blocking the way up, which require a bit of scrambling. In some places, the rock has been worn smooth, almost like tree roots. Huge ferns grow at the side of the path, like out of a dinosaur Triassic age. Halfway up, we spot Petit Piton, the sister rock, emerging from the peninsula of the coastline which snakes below. The shore is lapped by the waters of the cove we left Boris behind in. We can even see the mist covered hills of Saint Vincent to the south across the sea.

At the top, we find large slabs of stone and sit for a while admiring the view, allowing our sore muscles to recharge.

The Saint Lucian countryside sprawls out below us, and we can see the coast for miles as it hugs the Caribbean Sea. We appreciate our view of the entire south end of Saint Lucia, farms and villages below on the corrugations of little slopes and valleys. I spy banana plantations, a reminder of where we are.

We begin the descent, acquiring different blisters from the ones we made on the way up, and arrive back sorer, and sweatier than we started out and even Howard is subdued, quieter than usual. Boris watches us swim our aches away off the beach and then paddle the dinghy back towards him, listing heavily on one side from the slow leak. The old brigadier gazes out to sea, then looks up at the mountains.

"Well, I think we should get that dinghy fixed. We need it for run 'ashores'.

He uses the parlance the Royal Navy use for trips.

"Head north in two hours gents, I fancy a dusk cruise," he says next.

He looks happy, and rubs his stump again. Looks like we're on the night shift.

## 48 NIGHT SAIL TO MARTINIQUE

I'm looking forward to a night sail through the Caribbean sea, in my happy space. It would have to be my favourite time on board in some ways.

"Martinique is 50 nautical miles to the north. It's not a hard sail, we can make it overnight," Boris says, from up top.

He glances at the sky and checks the Shipping forecast.

Martinique is known as the "Pearl of the Antilles". This will be the northern extent of my trip; we are about 300 miles north-east of South America at that apogee. The island has a French or Creole-speaking population, and is part of the Windward chain. We'd have to sail to Dominica, next in the chain, to break the confines of the Windwards and reach the Leeward Islands.

We have an evening meal—a huge omelette with Cheddar and Red Leicester cheese, which Larry divides up, as we watch the sun dip towards the sea where it sends a long ray of sun light on to the sea near Anse Chastanet. There's an acute oblong of golden white light as it settles on the horizon for seconds before slipping under the waters. It is twilight for a bit longer, and the sky changes colour by degrees before it is dusk, then dark.

Howard flicks on the cockpit light once we've seen the show.

We prepare to get under way, which is securing a rope, and putting on a t-shirt and having a fleece to hand. Boris takes the wheel with one hand, his hook resting on the compass housing. We are in the stern watching—winding down the clock, making the occasional comment. It's still and balmy, with an accompanying breeze. We're on an easy beam reach, boom and sail out to our right, with the wind coming in from the east.

For a while, there seems to be no one around—but another boat flits past at some point, going in the opposite direction, port and starboard running lights on. There's not a sound from it, and no voices come across the water between us.

"It's quiet, isn't it?" notes Larry. "Bit unnerving in a way."

*Warrior* is lying off Martinique by 2 am, not a bad run.

Skipper hands down our watches, and we note our allocated times. I score the 1 am watch, and am in bed by 4 am, snoozing soundly.

When I awake at 8:30am, I feel I've caught the sun a bit. I notice a tint of red atop my tan, yet the skin under my watch strap is pale and clammy. Through the porthole, I can see we are approaching land, and I jump up, alarmed I might have overslept and missed anything.

Fort-de-France is our destination, the capital, where else—in a bay. To get there, the chart tells us we need to sail past a peninsula that juts out to the west. Overlooking the bay is an immense hill, almost volcanic in shape. My impression of a volcano is not misguided —the guide tells me this is Mount Pelée, an active volcano, 1,500 metres high. Gentler slopes run about half-way up through lightly forested land, parts of it cultivated by the looks of it. The final prominence is sheer and foreboding, a sort of tropical Tolkien Mordor.

We moor in the marina, and I remember we are essentially in France; an overseas department. The island is organised into arrondissements just like Paris. It's not in nature a former Overseas Dependency, or Territory as those of the UK. In the early 1980s, not everyone born in a UK island got UK citizenship after a law change, but people born in Martinique are as French as anyone in Marseille. Also in the Francophone world— islands like New Caledonia in the Pacific are also quintessentially French.

Tens of yachts are at their moorings, and people trek along the walkways, and lounge in cafes with their newspapers. I spot the chandlery store I assume Boris has in mind. A rowing boat slips past. The low monotone, even staccato, of French voices can be heard from boats and onshore.

Howard pops an unfinished apple in his mouth, pops the valve from the dinghy, and kneels on top of it. It deflates into a rubberized mangle, and he lies on it and wrestles with it to fold it so that two of us can carry it.

We walk in the sunlight down the quay. I am delighted to spy further icons of the French high street—a patisserie and boulangerie. The patisserie serves coffee, and I hear the sound of a barista clobbering the side of the coffee grounds bin with the *espresso* portafilter. My smile deepens when I notice locals leaving the boulangerie with *pain* in paper bags, often two or three in one go. Other reminders of France—there are three Renault sedans parked outside a blue façade.

Boris leads the way to the chandlery he knows. Outside, we spot a wooden placard advertising boat services and marine repair, and a mechanic is standing next to it. I glance up. There's a little boutique above all the industry and noise of repairs. There are cardboard cut-outs of girls modelling swimwear in the first-floor windows.

The proprietor is just inside the entrance, in front of a motor launch. He has a cigarette in his mouth, and his hands are black with oil and cigarette tar (Boris doesn't take up his offer to shake hands). Skipper enquires about a repair, and leads with the conversation, us boys listening in to the exchange, not as fluent in the vernacular as he clearly is.

"So, we've got a leak in our dinghy," he starts in simple French.

"I will have your boat ready tomorrow morning. It's a plug, yes?" replies the proprietor.

"A patch, yes, that will be fine. Beaucoup," intones Boris.

As we are in France, we might as well behave like Frenchmen, and we treat ourselves to a steak dinner in a non-pretentious bistro that doesn't need theming up, located in a cobbled street over from the chandlery. Boris orders us each a cognac after our dessert, and beckons the waiter over to enquire about the cigar collection. I can imagine him in the mess in Knightsbridge, on London public duties, with his company commanders and subalterns.

"Over to Bequia tomorrow," crows Skipper, and he nods at the waiter for the bill. "*L'addition*," he asks.

*The summing up.*

## 49 FIT FOR A PRINCESS

I stretch out in my berth for'ard and for a second, I can't work out where I am *again*—whether I am back in London, or not. The gentle rocking of *Warrior* reminds me we're afloat and I'm not in my bed in the UK, but in a berth of a small ocean-going vessel. I see Howard is up, cooking breakfast, fumigating the cabin. He pushes back his glasses on the bridge of his nose and smells the aroma contentedly.

Larry emerges from his berth opposite mine.

"Got mushrooms, Skipper?" Howard asks.

Boris indicates a corner cupboard to the rear.

"Hey–that smells good," Larry says.

I pop the kettle on the second ring, and when it sings, we sit down to sausages and bacon and a cup of Earl Grey.

*Bequia*. I had never heard of the place. I knew Barbados, Saint Lucia, courtesy of this trip. I also knew Bermuda (not so close to the Caribbean Sea) and Jamaica, but not this destination. It's a tiny isle—pronounced 'Beck-way' to the south of Saint Vincent, snuggled in a little chain of islands, a drop in the ocean. It is only seven square miles, long and narrow, and a popular destination for Christmas amongst yachties, and where Boris plans to spend his. Port Elizabeth is the safe harbour of choice. It's also known for where Princess Margaret, the Queen's sister, stayed later in life—she owned land on nearby Mustique where she lived with her gardener boyfriend.

It seems incredible that Grenada, the tiny little island invaded by the US Marines in 1983, lies a mere 150 miles to the south. Yet now, over ten years on, all appears quiet in this corner of the Caribbean. The fact the island is less known is surely what makes it so appealing.

We spend time cruising back down to Saint Lucia. Once we reach the southern tip, there's only 25 miles of open sea to rush across to get to Saint Vincent. You'd wonder if we need to look left and right before crossing. Here, winds can come rustling in off the Atlantic, but today winds are manageable. We observe the entire coast of sleepy Saint Vincent on our port side as it slips past us, mile by mile. Larry gets a Corona from the icebox he is resting his feet on, and pulls the ring on the can and stares out at the treed shoreline at the parrots, his arms hanging over the rail, looking pensive.

At long last, we cross the next gap between Saint Vincent and Bequia and spy our destination ahead of us, a sliver of real estate in the sea. I remind myself barely 5,000 people live here.

We stop up in the bay, allowing *Warrior* to drift on to anchor, which catches on the silted bottom, and row over to the jetty for a visit to customs.

There's a ubiquitous horseshoe-shaped bay with one-storey buildings. Again, the locals have been out with paint pots. There are two hangar-sized sheds on a jetty, with roofs painted in parrot-green, with gables gone over from a palette of yellows and lilacs. To compete the technicolor palette, one cyan building has a red tin roof, practical in tropical storms or hurricanes. The surrounding hinterland is forested and rises to steep hills. A road snakes along the shore.

Fishing dinghies bob up and down in the breeze, thirty metres out from the shore with a mooring line taken around a palm tree, all the way across the water. I spot a large skinny pier on stilts stretching out to the lagoon. The shore end meets the entrance of a sheltered church graveyard.

Otherwise, we could be in any port in the world, even back in Scotland.

I join Boris for breakfast and a chat over the papers—he's delighted to see a copy of the *Daily Express* on the table, a few days old, and insists on it being his treat. I enjoy a serving of eggs Benedict, and he has a full English breakfast. We share a pot of tea. The discussion moves on to career moves, and I explain I have a job with the Army back in the UK, and he talks about life in a calvary reconnaissance unit.

"Have you thought about it?" he asks.

We walk along sun-dappled roads past cafes and a bakery in port and find a bar in the early afternoon overlooking the bay.

## 50 ISLAND HOPPING FOR CHRISTMAS NIGHT

It's time for me to take leave of my third crew and head back to Saint Lucia, and I will travel back through the island chain we have sailed, by ferry, then small plane. I can travel from Bequia, to Kingstown, Saint Vincent, and then to Saint Lucia in a mere skip and a hop.

The scarlet-coloured ferry leaves Port Elizabeth in the morning. It's not large, with a cabin to the stern, and everyone stands in a flat area like in a Second World War landing craft. It's mostly locals, not many tourists at all, so I must stand out a fair bit. I position myself near a gantry mounted in the bow where cargo can be hoisted aboard. It's only an hour to Saint Vincent on the 'main' land, nine miles away.

Kingston, the capital, is of course quite a bit bigger than Port Elizabeth, with two-storey buildings stretching back to the wooded slopes. There's a more serious looking, five-storied building framed by two towers. The *Rough Guide* says the town is home to about ten thousand people. A fire truck swishes past, lights and sirens off.

I stroll up the shore from the ferry port looking for accommodation and find a room in a bed and breakfast. It has a colonial vibe and a stucco clad exterior. Pillars support a verandah with balustraded railing from the office to the bedrooms. The room has crisp sheets, a nightstand and a whirring ceiling fan, and a garden accessible from the room. I choose a paperback from a bookcase and read for an hour, sneezing as I turn the dust-afflicted pages.

*** 

I've got a flight to catch.

The Caribbean is served by its own airline: Leeward Islands Air Transport Services (LIAT). The guidebook can't wait to tell me it's also known as "Leave Island Any Time", a commentary on its reliability. It flies the island chains from Haiti, looping down as far south to Trinidad off the coast of Venezuela.

The waiting plane is a small turboprop design, and two young, handsome officers sit in the cockpit, in short sleeves, wearing Ray-Ban Wayfarers. They look ice-cool, as befits a pair with a plum job. With a smooth motion, one advances the throttle forward towards the instrument panel and we gather speed down the runway. They are game enough to leave their cockpit door open so sitting behind them, I can see through the windshield at approaching Saint Lucia as we hop between the isles.

A lone woman sits with me as cabin crew, and beams when she announces landing is about to commence. There's not much for her to do other than look the part on our descent. The boys in the front are busier, and adopt a manner of studied concentration as they line up on the runway.

We land at regional Vigie airport with no fuss, flying low over the heads of holidaymakers sunning themselves on the beach. Leaving the turboprop behind on the tarmac, I head through a tunnel to a taxi which can take me straight to Hewanorra International Airport near Vieux-Fort. There is no time to have a look anywhere or do anything. The check in for the charter to London Gatwick opens soon. It's eight hours non-stop.

I get talking to a girl my age and her parents in the departure lounge, but we are interrupted by feedback from the loudspeaker when a member of the cabin crew presses the switch on the PA.

"Ladies and Gentlemen, we are announcing the delay of Flight 22 to London Gatwick. Please wait in the lounge for further information as it comes to hand: we apologise for any inconvenience caused," intones the representative.

We'll be going nowhere.

"Of course," murmurs an older gent sitting nearby.

He throws his arms up, and there is a collective sigh of dismay from the passengers.

I stand up, stretch my legs and sit back down on my bag, not too concerned.

We learn Flight 22 to London Gatwick is not just delayed, it's not departing today at all. The problem is technical difficulties. The emergency floor lighting won't turn on, which seems trivial maybe—right until you need it. The airline says it is waiting for spares to be flown out from Florida, but they will put us up in a hotel for the night.

After weeks away, it's no drama for me. I have plenty of time on my hands, I've got no job to perform or career to pursue. For others, it's a huge inconvenience; those who have connections to make, or firm Christmas plans. For the young 'uns on the passenger manifest, it suits us fine to have another night accommodated at someone else's expense.

*Make hay whilst the sun shines.*

We are pleased to see the hotel is rated five-star. The staff allocates rooms sensibly—boy with boy, girl with girl—I am sharing with an older man in his fifties. But perhaps more encouragingly—drinks will be on the house. The bright young things bussed back to the hotel with me accompany me to the bar where we work our way through the cocktail list.

I quietly enter the room at 2 am, as best I can. I sink to the floor next to the double bed so as not to wake my roommate. He is embarrassed about privacy, but we are in this mess together.

"Come to bed," he says, more awkwardly than he intended, and draws open the covers.

I pick myself up from the floor and tuck in next to him.

Come the morn, Christmas Eve, the Airbus is finally fit to fly, but not before we've had a large buffet breakfast. It's not strictly an "all you can eat buffet, but I treat it as one: I enjoy cereal, fresh fruit and move on to bacon and eggs, washed down with sugary fruit juice that will take the enamel off my teeth. I'm definitely full, I realise, as I board the minibus to the airport.

The charter flight rotates off the main runway and heads out over the Atlantic pointing back towards a European winter and Christmas night.

## 51 BACK IN BLIGHTY

We land on Christmas morning. The UK is cold, no surprise there, and I can see no sign of Christmas at arrivals. My fellow travellers must be desperate to get home after the delay.

I recover my pack from the baggage reclaim after a brief wait. I smell a distinctive odour of fish oil when I hoist it to my shoulders—someone's precious delicacy they have secreted in the hold out of the eyes of prying customs has leaked from their bag, at my inconvenience.

I exit the terminal in my t-shirt, shorts, and boat shoes, figuring I'll be on the night bus before long, but my lack of planning means I will pay it forward when I wait for the bus. My feet are cold, and I shudder involuntarily in the night. It's not freezing, but at three degrees above, it might as well be, and I curse at my stupidity for not bringing a jumper. The driver on overtime nonetheless looks glum, not the welcoming Caribbean local I have become accustomed to, and I'm reminded my adventure is over. It's time to come back down to earth.

I travel to my father's house in London, splashing out on a taxi from the station, mulling over the events of the last six weeks. My father, and twin brother greet me enthusiastically, and I drop my gear off in the hall to see a table with Christmas breakfast, a glass of wine and fruit.

"Happy Christmas Steve," he announces. "How was it?"

"I'll tell you all about it, Dad," I reply, and sink down on to the sofa, legs up.

The blinding blue sky of the Caribbean Sea is still in my head and the dull light and overcast skies of London can't yet dispel that lovely vision. But the turkey and the hot pudding with cream, custard and brandy, goes down a treat and sticks to my insides reassuringly. The Queen's speech is on TV at 3 pm and we raise a glass.

What's next on the plan?

A stint with the Army, only this time in an office in the planning section of the main headquarters down in Wiltshire. It's a "Joint" HQ which means its Army, Navy and Royal Air Force. Maybe it's an apt, quiet, restraining grasp on the wrist if you like —a levy, or final dues owing, after a year on land and sea.

I pack a holdall, and get a room in barracks. It's still cold— the UK sits in a snap of temperatures that are below zero at breakfast. I press green working uniform with the iron set on maximum steam, and report to the office and the captain I will be working for.

It's a narrow, long room of desks with a panel of colonels, commodores and group captains wearing green, blue and light blue. I sit in an office at the end, presiding over a safe for my "Confidential" files which I unlock in the morning and secure at close of business. I perk up when a girl on base asks about my suntan and parachute wings, and comes over to sit with me at breakfast.

As is often the case, there was one more final amusing anecdote to come.

In the spring of 1996, I get a job with a small boutique consulting company. It's based on the Southampton road over the county line in Hampshire. I rent a room in a shared Victorian town house and accept a lift from a colleague every morning. He picks me up in a layby near an Esso service station.

One weekend, I stroll down there for a coffee. As I wait in line with people waiting to pay for their petrol, I bump into Larry coming through the doorway. Our mouths drop open at the same time—we must look a sight. The last time I had seen him five months ago, he was leaning over the gunwale of *Warrior* waving madly, three thousand nautical miles away, and here we were, only a mile from my digs.

"What are you doing here, Steve?" he asks, incredulously.

"I might ask you the same question," I reply. "How have you

been, mate?"

We shake hands.

And almost 30 years later, at the bottom of my drawer, I still have a pristine white ARC t-shirt largely unworn. But in fact, as I write these words, I am wearing it. It fits perfectly.

# GLOSSARY

Aft — Back eg "aft of where you are standing"

ARC — Atlantic Rally for Cruisers an event held since 1985

"Bearing away" — steering the boat before a gybe (the stern passes through wind)

Beating — sailing into the wind

Boom — metal pole which extends from the mast towards back of boat

Cleat — A metal anchor to secure a sheet from a sail to the deck to tie it off

Close-hauled — sailing into the wind, sail close to the mast

Company — about 100 men or women in an infantry company

Dartmouth — the Royal Navy Training college for officers

For'ard — Forward – the front of the boat

Foresail — Front sail (before the mast)

Fore — Front

Forestay — A pole from mast on which foresail is attached

Gib — Small foresail

Genoa — Larger foresail

Gunwale — Top edge of a boat

Gybing — Turning the stern through the wind. The boom comes over automatically.

Halyard — A line to pull on to haul up a sail

"Luffing Up" — turning the wheel to tack and change course — the wind drops out of the sail as the boat gets close to the wind

Mainsail — Main sail

Masthead — Top of the mast

Mooring — A place for a boat to tie up at

Painter — A line to pull or tow a boat, used perhaps when mooring

Platoon — About 30 men or women in an infantry company

Port — Nautical term for Left

Running (before the wind) — sailing with the wind behind

Sheet — A rope attached to a sail to control it.

Sloop — A yacht with one mast (that would be most..)

Spinnaker — Large front sail to catch the wind when running in front of the wind

Starboard — Nautical term for Right

Tacking — Turning the front of the boat through the wind to get on to the other tack

## PHOTOS OF A YEAR ON LAND AND SEA

For photos of the book, and to see other books
by Stephen Malins,  see author's website

stephenmalinsauthor.com

# RAH RAH AND ROOS : FARMING AND TRAVEL IN THE GREAT SOUTHERN LAND [THE NO #1 BEST SELLER]

Is it time you ditched the office and headed to the outback of Australia for the adventure of a lifetime? In 2002, a young Englishman did just that.

One year, 2,000 sheep: 4,000 km travelled. He uncovered real life far from the hustle and bustle of the beaches and coffee shops of the East coast. He learned to fly and worked on sheep and cattle stations, passed a truck test by the skin of his teeth - and toiled out in the gold fields in 40 degree heat.

Available on Amazon

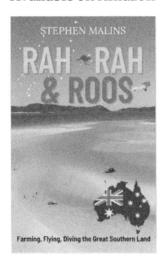

## ACKNOWLEDGEMENT

I'd like to thank Dawne Archer, Liza Grantham, Gary Gaunt, Tammy Horvath, Jackie Lambert, Chris Moore, Simon Michael Prior, Irene Pylypec and Alison Ripley-Cubitt for their assistance with my manuscript, and all those who can't be, (or would rather not be) named for their kind encouragement.

Also, to my darling wife Kiki, and children, who put up with my excitement and talking about it too much, as yet another book took shape some 30 years after events.

## ABOUT THE AUTHOR

Years later, Steve now lives in Melbourne, Australia, with his wife and three teenagers. As such, he is an unpaid uber-driver.

He works in an office for his many sins, but volunteered as a Country Fire Authority firefighter and loves getting out in the High Country and on skis in the Australian Alps.

# COPYRIGHT

Printed in Great Britain
by Amazon

39117375R00128